Tales of
WATCHET HARBOUR

Watchet is a small seaport on the Somerset Coast. It has an intriguing history which goes back a thousand years. Many stories of the harbour and its ships and sailors have sporadically been put into print by various well known authors. Other tales, perhaps best described as harbour lore, have been handed down verbally through generations of local seafaring families. Some of these tales indeed, were related first hand to the writer by the very men who manned the last of Watchet's fine sailing fleet.

This book is an attempt to collect many of these fast disappearing tales, legends and odd bits of doggerel, and to present them as near as possible in chronological order.

Part one deals mainly with the development of the harbour from the time of the Vikings to the present day. It also gives the story of the long struggle for survival of the small harbour town community.

Part two features some of the ships and the men who sailed in them. They were men of great courage, skill and endurance.

Lifeboatmen, fishermen, shipwrights and harbourside characters have been included, for they too, are part of the harbour story.

'The Home Port of the Ancient Mariner'

Painting of Watchet Harbour c. 1708

(By courtesy of the Wyndham family)

Tales of
WATCHET HARBOUR

(THE SOMERSET PORT OF A THOUSAND YEARS)

THIRD EDITION

W. H. (Ben) Norman

W H Ben Norman.

Published by
W. H. (Ben) Norman
LYN COTTAGE · MILL LANE · WATCHET
SOMERSET · TA23 0AR

First published 1985
Reprinted 1988
Completely revised and reprinted 2002
© W. H. (Ben) Norman
ISBN 0 9510842 0 8

ACKNOWLEDGEMENTS

Many people have given information, or have helped me in other ways to produce this book, and to them I am most grateful.

In particular I would like to thank Dr. Basil Greenhill, former Director of the National Maritime Museum; Derek Shorrocks *(County Archivist, and staff of the Somerset Record Office)*; Gareth Purcell *(Editor, and staff of the West Somerset Free Press)*; David Bromwich *(Somerset Local History Library)*; Miss Perry *(Curator, R.N. Hydrographic Department)*; David Greenfield *(Somerset Industrial Archaeological Society)*; Edna Dixon *(My sister)*; William Norman *(My cousin)*; Fred Bacon; Ernest Binding; Howard Burton; Robin Madge; Charles Hadfield; Michael Bouquet; Dr Katherine Wyndham; Mrs T. Farthing; Jan Ridler; Percival Risdon; Derek Quint; Jack Binding; Capt. Tom Ley; Capt. Christofell Muller; Colin and Mrs Connett; Vernon Stone; John O'Connor; Leslie Wedlake; Michael Sully; Michael Ireland; John Gilman; Graham Coggins; David Proctor; John Stengelhoffen; Jack Duddridge; Dr Robert Dunning; Rodger Sellick; Peter Hesp; Dick Norman; Dr Glyn Court; Paul Norton; Geoffrey Roberts; Mrs Elsie Farr; Stuart McMillan; Capt. Leslie Morrish; also to S. R. (Bob) Pope of Exeter, who was of great help to me in getting this book finally into print.

I would also like to mention here three friends now deceased, who gave me a great deal of information and encouragement: Jack Hurley, John H. Norman and Captain James Dew.

Front cover:

Topsail Schooner, *Louise.* Original painting by Thomas Chidgey — Master Mariner and Marine Artist of Watchet.

Back cover:

The lovely Ketch *Irene* — Built in Somerset 1907 and still sailing in 1988.
(By courtesy of Capt. Leslie Morrish, owner)

Photograph by Photomarine Services of Wimborne, Dorset (Tel: 0202 — 889438)

Designed by Nigel R. Pope

Humorous drawings by Derek Quint

Printed and bound by Short Run Press Ltd, Exeter.

Contents

PART ONE

PART TWO

Dedication

To my father Capt. Frank Norman and all the Master Mariners and Sailors of Watchet in the days of sail.

Foreword

Ben Normans delightful "Tales of Watchet Harbour" is not only very good reading it is a useful contribution to the maritime history of South West Britain. Mr. Normans' work has the authority of intimate local knowledge of the community in which he lives and this is combined with a working knowledge of merchant shipping matters which gives his book both interest and authority.

I am very pleased indeed that it is being published and will now be available to a wider readership.

BASIL GREENHILL
Former Director of the National Maritime Museum, London

Bibliography

Wreck and rescue in the Bristol Channel	*Grahame Farr*
Somerset Harbours	*Grahame Farr*
No gallant ship	*Michael Bouquet*
Westcountrymen in Prince Edward Island	*Basil Greenhill & Ann Gifford*
Snow and storm on Exmoor	*Jack Hurley*
West Somerset Mineral Railway	*Rodger Sellick*
History of part of West Somerset	*Chadwick Healy*
History of Minehead	*Hancock, Preb. H.*
A tour through the Island of Great Britain	*Daniel Defoe*
William Jessop, Engineer	*Charles Hadfield & A. W. Skempton*
Anglo Saxon Chronicle	
The Wyndham papers	*Somerset Record Office*
Minute books of Watchet Harbour Commissioners	*Somerset Record Office*
Minute books of Watchet Urban District Council	*Somerset Record Office*
West Somerset Free Press, 1860–1984	

Many of the photographs within this publication were taken by the early photographers: James Date and Bert Hole of Watchet, and H. H. Hole of Williton.

The Author

The author, William Henry (Ben) Norman, was born in 1918 into a family long established in the coasting trade and was reared on stories of Watchet Harbour and its ships and sailors.

As a boy he occasionally sailed with his father aboard the *Charlotte*, one of the last of the port's fine fleet of sailing ships, also with Captain Reuben Chichester on the ketches *Bonita* and *Democrat* of Braunton, North Devon. For some years the writer owned and operated a fishing and pleassure boat from the harbour and was a member of the Hobblers Association (men who assist in berthing and mooring ships).

For a few years he served on the harbour committee of the Town Council and is a founder member and Hon Curator of Watchet Museum being involved in its unique collection of maritime artefacts.

Part One

Watchet's first sailor

CHAPTER 1

914-1745
THE EARLY DEVELOPMENT OF THE HARBOUR

The earliest Harbour or landing place at Watchet was almost certainly of natural formation and was probably situated in the mouth of the small river which here joins the sea.

Even to this day, were it not for a long culvert and bridge built over the river, small vessels could navigate some way upstream at high tide. To give extra protection from the prevailing Westerly winds, a single mole or break-water would have been constructed.

A legendary tale has often been told of a Welshman who must have been one of the earliest sailors to sail into Watchet harbour. His name was Decuman and he is reputed to have sailed across the Bristol Channel from Wales on a hurdle accompanied by a cow. He took up residence on a hill overlooking the harbour and quietly set about building a Christian Church.

Local folk for no known reason took a dislike to him and chopped off his head. Being a Saint, he was quite undismayed and calmly took his head to a nearby Holy well, after washing it he popped it on again and proceeded to complete the building of the first Parish Church of Saint Decuman's.

Some visiting sailors in the year 914 AD were very unwelcome indeed, for they were the dreaded Vikings. Led by two Earls they had sailed in their longboats from the coast of Brittany.

They stole inland at night to the east of the town, then set about looting, raping, and burning the place down. Greatly enraged Watchetites mounted a successful counter attack and the invaders were driven back to the sea. Only those who could swim out to their boats escaped with their lives. They hastily set sail to their temporary stronghold on the island of Steepholm and later sailed off to Ireland.

Some 74 years later in 988 AD the Vikings again invaded Watchet in far greater numbers, and yet again in 997. On both of these occasions great slaughter and burning took place.

The reason the Vikings had picked on Watchet was because it was at this time a place of considerable importance, having its own mint. Silver pennies were being produced and it is believed that the Vikings must have had considerable success in their raids, for in later years large hoards of Watchet pennies were discovered in Scandinavian countries.

1

King Alfred is believed to have paid much of his tribute money *"Danegeld"* in Watchet coinage.

A brief and early reference to the harbour mentions that King Henry III sent a message to the Sheriff of Somerset (c. 1250) telling him he had heard of the landing of certain merchandise at Watchet to the detriment of Dunster, and ordered that a stop should be put to this.

(Note: There was probably a naturally formed harbour at Dunster at this time, in the mouth of the little river Aville, which has long since been silted up).

Watchet's little breakwater and most of its buildings were almost destroyed by storms in 1458.

Urgent appeals for help were sent to Bishop Bekynton of Wells Cathedral. The wily Bishop did not send immediate cash aid. Seemingly he believed in the old adage "Charity begins at home". He was, however, a dab hand at fund raising gimmicks and accordingly instructed all friars and Ecclesiastics of his Diocese to grant *FORTY DAYS INDULGENCE* to all contrite and confessed persons who would contribute to Watchet harbour repairs, *AFTER* they had contributed to the maintenance of Wells Cathedral. (No record exists of the amount contributed by the laity or what they might have indulged in for forty days.)

An early industry at Watchet was the weaving of woollen cloth and packs of this commodity were at intervals shipped away. Said to have been dyed from the juice of locally grown whortleberries, it was known as Watchet Blue.

Uniforms of Watchet Blue were supplied for Sir Hugh Willoughby's ill-fated expedition to China. Sir Hugh in command of three ships left London in 1553 seeking a new North East passage to China. After encountering terrible weather which caused great delay, part of the expedition took shelter in Arzinia, a Lapland harbour and decided to winter there. Despite their warm Watchet woollen clothing, they were ill-equipped to withstand the rigours of an Arctic Winter and they perished, every one. Another ill-fated wearer of this material was King Charles I who went to the scaffold attired in a waistcoat of Watchet Blue.

England was under threat of invasion in 1544 and a plan was prepared showing proposed anti Invasion Defences along the Somerset coast. This plan from the Cottonian MSS, the original of which is in the British Library, shows gun site positions at Minehead and Combwich and two forts with cannon at Porlock. Three ships are shown at Watchet sheltering behind some sort of weir, or semi-circular enclosures of piles.

A copy of the plan is on view at Watchet Museum.

A report by a Royal Commission in 1566 which inquired into the state of the Port of Bridgwater noted of Watchet, which was within the precinct of that Port: "Where small botes have and do use to come yn with salte, Wyne, vyctualles, wood and coole."

In or about the year 1608 Thomas Salkeld — a notorious and cruel pirate —

2

had taken possession of Lundy Island in the Bristol Channel. From this stronghold, with a gang of cut-throats, he plundered innocent passing merchant ships and lived like an Emperor feasting and drinking on stolen victuals. He either killed the crews of the merchant ships or took them prisoner and treated them as slaves. George Eskott, a Watchet sailor on a ship from Bridgwater, was captured and imprisoned on Lundy. George was a believer in law and order and took a poor view of Salkeld and his cruel louts. He bided his time — then led a revolt overpowering Salkeld and his drunken rogues, and delivered them to justice. A grateful King James I thanked George and awarded him a pension of 18 pence a day.

During the Civil War (early 1600s) a Royalist ship from Wales became stranded on a ridge of pebbles off the harbour at Watchet. Cromwellian troopers under the command of Captain Popham rode their horses breast-deep into the water to attack. By this means they were able to get near enough to fire their carbines and wrought such havoc that the ship surrendered. The incident was set down in an account of the life of Sir Robert Blake as: "the greatest rarity of all — that a ship on the sea was taken by a troop of horse."

The observant writer, Gerard of Trent, walking through Somerset in 1633 wrote — WATCHET which ye Saxons called Waced port and which ye Danes in ye years of our Lord 888 robbed and burned, a little harbour it hath in ye mouth of a Riverette which here falleth into ye sea .... wence divers take shipping to Ireland.

The names of seven Watchet ships are recorded in Hancock's History of Minehead which gives a list of ships trading to Minehead in 1647 including:

> George of Watchet, John Torrington.
> Hart of Watchett, John Priest, jun.
> Grace of Watchett, John Priest.
> Speedwell of Watchett, Rob. Hooper.
> Costley of Watchet.
> Garland of Watchet.
> Black Boule of Watchet — Dashwood.

Yet more damage was caused by storms in 1659 & 1661 for records at the Church of Compton Bishop in Somerset mention that the sum of 3/6 was collected for the reparation of the key or pier at Watchet. Several other churches in various parts of the country also contributed including St. Christopher Le Stocks, which stood on a part of the site now occupied by the Bank of England Here 22 shillings was raised for "Ye repair of ye Peere and harbour of Watchplott."

Most of the trade through the harbour at that time was the import of coal and salt and the export of KELP — a variety of seaweed which was used at

Bristol for glass bottle making. GYPSUM – a type of alabaster was dug from nearby cliffs and shipped away for the manufacture of Plaster of Paris.

Chadwick Healy, in his "History of part of West Somerset", gives us details of another flourishing but unauthorised trade; in 1682 a great deal of smuggling was taking place at Watchet. So much so that Charles II sent his Surveyor General of Customs – one Culliforde – to report back to him. Culliford found and reported that William Dashwood, the local collector of customs, spent most of his time in a Watchet pub called The Blue Anchor drinking 'sack' with the captains of the ships, and whilst he was thus engaged cargoes of wine and brandy were run ashore without any duty being paid. What is more the Lord of the Manor, Sir William Wyndham, patronised the townsfolk in all their actions and Watchet, from being a town of beggars had, within ten years, grown exceedingly rich and that Watchet now had as large a trade as Minehead. Dashwood's assistant Perry, obviously with an eye to promotion, turned informer and Culliford also discovered that some ships did nothing else other than run illicit goods. One Ambrose Webber, not involved in the smuggling, was said to have endeavoured to disturb the persons that were running the goods by setting his dog on them, at which action the said Mr. Dashwood was very angry and called him "Damned Rogue" for endeavouring to disturb the persons running the said goods. Also implicated was one Robert Hooper (Jnr). He was reported to have loaded 5 or 6 tons of wine and brandy from his ship the *Industry*.

No duty had been paid and when challenged by the Kings Officers, Hooper and his rascally crew had drawn swords and cheekily sailed away.

Morgan Byneham, master of the ship *Adventure* of which John Woolcots of Tolland was part owner, was laden with wine, brandy, lynnen cloth and salt. The salt entered and paid duty at Mynehead but the wine brandy and cloth was all run, and was a very considerable parcel, for there was not less than 30 men at work, between 2 & 3 hours delivering the same and all that while Mr. Dashwood was drinking sack with the master at the "Shipp" tavern.

William Dashwood, not surprisingly, was suspended and his job was taken over by his former assistant Perry. Culliford's report includes the wry comment "And for as much as the said Mr. Perry for making the discovery and doeing the King's service has begotten himself a general hatred throughout the town of Watchett."

Most of the remains of the old river-mouth harbour, due to storms and constant erosion, have long since disappeared. But in the writer's opinion and while admitting that it is only conjecture.

The small tidal basin on the South side of Market Street could be the inner part of the old original harbour, referred to by Gerard of Trent in 1633. This is easier to contemplate if one bears in mind that the Mineral Yard, which today covers the outer part of the river, was open beach until claimed from the sea in 1855. Furthermore the stone bridge over the river in Market Street, according to Mr.C.J.Phippen, who wrote to the West Somerset Free Press in Nov. 1938, was planned and constructed by a forebear of his in the early 1800's. Before the bridge was built, according to the same correspondent, a ford was in use at this particular point.

That constant erosion has taken place at Watchet is indicated in an early guide to Watchet which mentions old fishermen's stories that a hamlet known as Easentown situated to the Eastward of the harbour was washed away by the sea and to their great dismay the Town's brewery was also engulfed.

Those who live near the harbour, even today, are aware of the constant erosion and the warning supposedly uttered by Old Mother Shipton, a Yorkshire soothsayer, i.e.

> "Watchet and Doniford shall be drowned,
> and Williton become a seaport town."

but no-one is losing any sleep over it.

In 1708 an Act of Parliament authorised Sir William Wyndham, the Lord of the Manor, to build a new harbour at Watchet, as the old one was almost

Sir William Wyndham who in 1682 turned a blind eye to Watchet's smugglers. *(By courtesy of the Wyndham family)*

completely destroyed by storms. This Act and subsequent Acts entitled him to collect dues at the new harbour and also at a place called the Blue Anchor and Cleeve Steps adjoining the said harbour, for a specified number of years.

An Article of Agreement between Sir William Wyndham Baronet of Orchard Wyndham and William Row Freemason of Bridgwater was signed on the 12th January of that year.

William Row agreed to build the new harbour within two years for "One thousand pounds of good and lawful money". Eight hundred pounds to be paid to him in £100 instalments as the work progressed, and Row also agreed to maintain the new work for twenty years from the date of completion. The final £200 was to be withheld for that period but 6% interest on this money was to be paid to Row at half yearly intervals.

The new harbour was to consist of a single arm which curved around in a semi-circle and was similar in shape to the harbours which exist today at Minehead and Clovelly and to that at Hartland Quay prior to its destruction in 1896.

The Agreement also stipulated that the pier was to be five hundred and fifty feet long and to be built of "Ruff stones". "The best and largest that can be gotten in or about Watchet." The outer wall on the seaward side to be fourteen feet thick at the bottom and eight feet on the top. The inner wall on the harbour side to be five feet thick at the bottom and three feet at the top, and the cross walls to be eighteen feet in length and three feet thick. The height of the pier to be two feet above the high water mark, on the inner side, but seven feet including the parapet on the seaward side. The new pier was duly built. Quay dues collected by the Water Bailiff in the three years 1712-1714 were just over £100 per annum.

Whether William Row ever collected his final £200 is not known and is doubtful for in 1720 Thos. Chedgey a mason quoted £136.5.0 to repair large cracks in the said key head as the same was in great danger of falling down.

Only a year later Thomas Chedgey agreed to "Take down the present head of the key at Watchett afore the length of ffifty foot, inwards from the said key head and to new build the said key head and extend or lengthen the same ffifty foot at least beyond its present length in a good workmanlike manner." The work was carried out at a cost of £280.

A beautiful picture of Sir William Wyndham's newly built Watchet Harbour hangs in one of the rooms at Orchard Wyndham — the Manor. Mr. George Wyndham (who died in 1982) kindly gave the writer permission to view the painting and to photograph it. He also authorised a photograph of a portrait of his ancestor Sir William Wyndham. The picture of this newly built harbour is shown as the frontispiece opposite the title page.

The painting of the harbour deserves careful study — it is unsigned and little was known of its origin by Mr. Wyndham.

Mr. Edward Selwood, the Curator of oil paintings at the National Maritime

Museum to whom a photograph of the painting was shown by the writer, dates it at around 1700 – according to the rig of the ships.

The Parish Church, the contours of the land and the shape of the fields are all easily recognisable, and confirms that much erosion has taken place since the painting was executed. The large number of houses depicted is puzzling, but a few seem to be recognisable. What appears at first to be three cattle near the house in the foreground, on closer inspection, prove to be pack-horses with panniers on their backs.

In 1714 many cargoes of wool from Ireland were being shipped through nearby Minehead harbour for use all over the West Country. Minehead Harbour at this time was an established Staple Port with Government appointed customs officers. Consequently it was authorised to handle the bulk of the lucrative merchandise from overseas, including many cargoes of wool from Ireland. Watchet, being a sub-port under Minehead's control was restricted to handling only mundane coastwise cargoes such as coal, salt and hides on which little duty or harbour dues were payable. Merchants from Tiverton and Bampton objected to the heavy fees charged for weighing the wool at Minehead Town Hall, and Parliament was petitioned to make Watchet also a Staple or Free Port, so that they could import their cargoes of wool through Watchet harbour instead of paying through the nose at Minehead. Counter petitions were sent in from the inhabitants of Minehead who naturally wished to retain the trade for themselves. They were supported by the Corporations of Taunton, Bridgwater and even Bristol.

Watchet is a very dangerous place for ships declared the Minehead folk and is a very incommodious dry harbour not having water in it unless at Spring tides, for a ship of above 15 or 20 tons.

Watchet's appeal failed and they remained a sub port of Minehead until 1834. In that year Minehead lost its status and together with Watchet became sub-ports of Bridgwater.

Daniel Defoe, the well-known author, visited Watchet in 1724. He was not very impressed with the new harbour. He considered it was not built high enough, nor was it of sufficient length to give adequate shelter to shipping. Whilst walking on the beach he was amazed to find large fossils embedded in the rocks; he had never seen anything like them before and was greatly puzzled at their formation. The fossils in the rocks can still be seen to this day.

1728

The actual site of the Blue Anchor public house referred to by Culliford, the Customs Inspector, in 1682 unfortunately cannot be pin-pointed but a clue is provided by some interesting documents at the Somerset Records Office. The most explicit is an account by Thos. Chedgey dated 1728, which indicates that it was situated "beside the slip" as follows:—

"An Acott of y Charges & expenses in lengthening & repairing the Slipp by the Blew Anker in Watchett for the more easy coming and going of the plows to and from the key at Watchett £14.1.9."

Included with the account was a bill from Richard Wheddon and Richard Escott of Doniford who each charged 10/- per day for hauling stones to repair the slip on plows (sledges) which were each pulled by a team of eight oxen, also a bill from Richard Greenslade and John Woodland who were paid £1.19.5. for lime used in the work.

A list of the workmen which also appears to have included boys and the amount each was paid is as follows:

Augt – 27

	£	s	d
My sel 15 days (Thos. Chedgey)	1	17	6
Harry Chedgey 12	1	4	0
Nelas Chedgey 11	1	2	0
Will Brayent 15	1	10	0
Ed Davey 12	1	4	0
Rich Dun 15	0	15	0
Will Croker 15	0	15	0
youn Dun 15 (Boy?)	0	11	3
Rob Parrott 9	0	9	0
John Owen 9	0	9	0
John Tayler 2	0	2	0
Thoms Tayler 2	0	2	0
John Cann 4	0	4	0
John Aldarman 4	0	4	0
John Morl 10	0	10	0
Rich Grifey 6	0	6	0
Ed Wales 4	0	4	0
A Hoss to carry sand 4 days	0	2	8
Paid for Beare for the men	0	7	0
	11	18	5

1746

The origin and story of Watchet Court Leet is well recorded and described in A. L. Wedlake's "History of Watchet".

Regarding the harbour, the court had the authority to levy certain additional dues on imports of coal and salt and a Portreve was appointed annually to collect the dues, some of which were used to cover the expenses of the court and the services provided by its officers.

Among the various offenders dealt with by the court, nagging wives and witches were strapped onto a ducking stool and immersed in the harbour.

Jurors and various officials of the court such as the Bailiff, Town Cryer, Inspectors of weights and measures, pig drivers and ale tasters etc. were summoned to attend annually at the Bell Inn where the business of the court was carried out and new officials appointed. Considerately a hearty dinner was provided for all by the current Portreve. Here is the Portreve's detailed account for the dinner in 1746.

The account of the vitals & dressing			
26 Oct. 1746	£	s	d
For a Rump of Beef	0	3	4
For a Surloyne of Beef	0	4	4
For a Leg of Mutton	0	2	0
For a Guse	0	2	0
For the pertatis	0	1	0
For the turnips	0	0	6
For Ounions & happels for sage	0	0	6
For piper vinigor & Mustord	0	0	6
For the Butter	0	1	6
For the Bred	0	1	6
For the Chees	0	1	6
For coles two dress ye Meat & Burne in the Rumes	0	3	0
For the candell light	0	1	6
For the tabacke & pipes	0	1	6
For nuts	0	0	3
For labour in dressing the Meat	0	2	0
	£1	7	11

(Query: Did the Portreve's arithmetic in £.s.d. enable him to make a shilling for himself?)

Watchet's Court Leet has survived and still meets annually to appoint its Portreeve and Jurors, Ale taster and Pig driver etc. These officers no longer have to carry out their duties, but as has been the custom for hundreds of years, they sit down after being sworn in, to a hearty meal of roast goose followed by hot punch and walnuts.

POSTSCRIPT

The Court Leet in 1987 elected ex Sgt. Major Alec Danby to the post of Town Crier. Attired in a Yeoman Green cloak and Tricorn hat he delivers public notices in a voice of pure gold.

CHAPTER 2

1746-1835

THE LIMESTONE TRADE AND
PLANS FOR HARBOUR IMPROVEMENT

The Lime Stone and Gypsum trade

The production of lime was a major and early industry. It was used exten-
sively for building purposes, and farmers also spread it in great quantity over
their fields. Dozens of lime kilns along the Somerset and Devon coasts needed
supplies of 'culm' (small coal) for firing the kilns, and many small Watchet
smacks and ketches were employed in this trade.

Kilns at and near Watchet could obtain blue lias (lime stone) for burning
from the adjacent beaches; this was usually collected and then carried by
panniered donkeys to the kilns.

Kilns at and to the westward of Minehead lacked an adequate supply of
lime stone and, therefore, had to have supplies brought to them by the
trading smacks as well as supplies of 'culm'. This lime stone was usually
obtained from the large deposits on the beaches at East Quantoxhead to the
east of Watchet or at ABERTHAW on the opposite side of the Bristol
Channel. Many of the kilns were situated on open beaches and the little
vessels supplying them were often in grave danger. The crew greatly feared
a change of wind whilst unloading their cargo into horse drawn carts — their
vessel being high and dry on the beach. Many were unable to beat off into a
strong onshore wind and were driven ashore and wrecked.

The lime produced at Watchet was quite famous. When used as a mortar
it had excellent bonding qualities and would set off rock hard — even under-
water. It was, therefore, in great demand for harbour or sea defence work.

In or about the year 1759, the eminent marine engineer — John Smeaton —
had the formidable task of building a new Lighthouse on the Eddystone
Rock near Plymouth. He ordered supplies of lime from Watchet which was
transported overland to Plymouth by pack-horses. Smeaton's lighthouse
tower gave many years of service. It was eventually replaced by a new one,
but the old Smeaton tower was dismantled and re-erected on Plymouth Hoe
where it still stands today.

Lime burning at Watchet ended in the 1940's — it's use in building had
been taken over by Portland Cement and although some farmers still use

lime on their fields, this is obtained from other sources where it is doubtless mass produced and delivered by road.

Gypsum was another material which was dug from the cliffs and shipped away for manufacture into plaster of Paris, or in later years for use in paper manufacture.

Parts of the foreshore near Blue Anchor known as *The Berths* were cleared of rocks and marked with tall posts to facilitate the mooring, berthing and loading of ships engaged in the hazardous trade.

One section of the cliffs from which the gypsum was quarried was known as *Chapel Pits*. This was once the site of a Chapel built by the monks of Cleeve Abbey. Due to the coastal erosion it has long since fallen into the sea.

Among the Wyndham papers at the Somerset Record Office are a couple of Freight Lists of various commodities which were shipped from Bristol consigned to the Lord of the Manor.

One of these lists dated 1727 includes:

5 Mauns of Lichers and a bage of corks

2 boxes of nails

a bundle of matts

a large marble ston

2 Mauns of Hotwellwater (note: possibly mineral water from Hotwells Spa)

3 Mauns of full botels and a cask and a box

(Note: A Maun is a large hamperlike basket).

Another Freight List dated 1732 also consigned to the Lord of the Manor includes:

4 tons of millstones

3 Chairs

A bundlle of mattins

A large box with glass and a Jar of oyle

A cask of blacksope and a barril of gunpowder
and a hundred and half of shott

A Barrel of Wine and a bage of Corks,

A maun of botels.

A list of goods shipped to Watchet from Bristol in 1750 included:

8 tons of groceries	2000 bricks
12 tons of iron	a Smiths bellas (Bellows?)
2 tons of clover seed	4 Grinding Stones
1½ tons of cheese	2 furnasses

11

A list of goods shipped to Bristol from Watchet in 1750 included:

602 sacks of corn	3 G Ox Bows
15 packs of cloth	2 tons of Elm Boards
15 tons of kelp (seaweed)	8 Dickers of leather
2 tons of wood ashes	6030 OX HORNS

The names of the ships which carried the above goods to and from Bristol in 1750 were the *Betty* and the *Susannah* owned by Mr. John Good.

It was about 1797 that the famous poet Samuel Taylor Coleridge visited Watchet accompanied by the equally famous Wordsworth and his sister Dorothy. It is widely believed that Coleridge was inspired after visiting the harbour and talking with the old sailors to write his 'Rime of the Ancient Mariner'.

> The ship was cheered – the harbour cleared
> Merrily did we drop – below the Kirk
> Below the hill – below the Lighthouse top.

By the year 1797 the harbour had come under the ownership of George O'Brien Wyndham, 3rd Earl of Egremont who was now the Lord of the Manor.

Henry Tripp was the steward for the Estate and therefore had control of the harbour. Correspondence between Henry Tripp and his brother J. Upton Tripp, a lawyer, indicates that once again plans were afoot to improve Watchet's harbour and hopefully these improvements would enable Watchet to be upgraded and made a "Free Port" and thus entitled to handle more varied and lucrative cargoes. Local Shipowners and Merchants petitioned the Earl to improve the harbour by building a new East pier (as follows):

11th SEPTEMBER 1797

The humble petition of the Merchant Traders and Shipholders of the Town and port of Watchett in the County of Somerset

To the Right Honourable the Earl of Egremont

Humbly Sheweth

That your petitioners suffering greatly in their Commerce from the ungovernable Rage of the Sea brought in the pier by the N Easterly winds which have not only proved fatal to many of the outbuildings but many ships have actually sunk in the Harbour when laden with valuable Merchandize to the very great injury of the Merchants and all concerned,

Now to remedy those evils complained of we the said Subscribers with all Submission beg leave to lay before your Lordship how great a thing it would be for the Commercial Interests of this place was your Lordship to cause a substantial Wall to be Errected that would stop the progress of the Sea from entering the pier with such violence the inside of the pier and all the exposed Walls and your Land would be secured, your petitioners that now watch their ships when this happen all night could then Sleep with comfort in their Beds, our Ships and Tackle would then last double the time they now do and the advantage that must accrue to your Lordship from the increase of Trade must be very considerable especially if we add the excellent Regulations lately made on the Turnpike Road leading to and from Taunton, Wiveliscombe, Bampton, Dulverton. It has caused a much greater demand for Coals than we ever had or possibly can now serve them with in our present situations.

Therefore should your Lordship on perusal of this concur in Sentiment with us your petitioners have only to add that as a considerable part of the Duty ariseing from the Merchandize of this place Contributes to the payments of Salarys in the Custom House of Minehead eight Miles distant from this port and this Journey we are obliged to take so often as we clear out for any other port these hardships your petitioners has laboured under for near a Century not having it in our powers to Ship a pack of goods of any sort after Clearing and except repeating the Journey over again and a second expense attending it and if a Ship Foreign is blown into this port and has goods to a large or small amounts the property of your petitioners they dare not Land or we Receive it till at a Staple port its Landed and returned to us in other Bottoms,

And now to conclude the sum of all we requests of your Lordship is for a N. East Wall as before mentioned and a Staple port Independent of Minehead.

Mather Wills	Francis Jenkins	John Williams
John Winter	Thomas Jenkins	William Crocker
Nicholas Tanner	William Pulman	Francis Hole
Lewis Winter	William Gimblett	Geen Stenner
T Welch	Marg't Gimblett	John Hurley
A Welch	John Melton	George Union
Robert Morle	John Sibley	James Wood
J Skinner	North & Bosley	Wm Wood
Totterdal & Hole	Thos Wheddon	Mary Owen
William Potter	Rich Wheddon	Nat Potter
		Wm Pearse

At this time the leading Harbour and Docks Engineer of the entire country was William Jessop who had himself been trained by the famous aforementioned engineer John Smeaton of Eddystone Lighthouse fame. Among William Jessop's great engineering accomplishments was the building of the West India Docks in London and Bristol's Floating Harbour as well as Ringsend Docks in Dublin. He was commissioned by the 3rd Earl of Egremont to make a report on Watchet harbour and to advise on improving it.

George O'Brian Wyndham, the 3rd Earl of Egremont.
(By courtesy of the Wyndham family)

William Jessop's report on Watchet Harbour to the Earl of Egremont and estimated cost of a new East Pier in 1797.

My Lord,

The Harbour of Watchet in its present state is formed by a small Bay or indenture in the Shore, sheltered from all Winds from the South between the East and Western Points by the Lands and from Winds between the West and Northern Points by a Pier 500 feet in Length; the Harbour is dry at low water, but the bottom being covered with Beach or Shingle, Vessels may take the Ground in Safety when the Water is not much agitated. But tho' the present Pier afford tolerable Protection from those Winds which bring the heaviest Seas into the Channel and which are also most generally predominant, the Harbour is totally open and exposed to many points between the North and East. In consequence very considerable inconvenience and annoyance is experienced by Vessels which must necessarily use the Port, and many others which would be glad to run in for shelter are deterred from doing so because they cannot expect certain Protection: I am informed that it frequently happens in Easterly winds that Vessels working up the Channel and failing in their attempt to reach their Port are under the necessity of running back to Minehead, because at such times they can have no shelter in the Harbour of Watchet.

For the foregoing Reason it is obviously desirable that this defect should be remedied and this may be effectually done by the projection of an Eastern Pier, the site for which is fortunately marked by a Ledge of Rocks, which tho' intermixt with Strata of marle will when covered make a safe foundation at a small Expense except towards the head of the Pier where it may be necessary to sink about 5 feet and at the Extremity of the Head rather more than that for the Foundation.

From the erection of the Pier will be derived the following important benefits.

It will with the other enclose a Space of near nine acres (except what must unavoidably be exposed to the Opening necessary for the free Entrance into and Departure from the Harbour) instead of something less than two Acres which is the Area of the present Harbour.

It will on either one side or the other give perfect Protection in all Winds to the Vessels which may enter either to take in or discharge their lading to others which may occasionally resort to the Port for Shelter.

It will consequently tend to considerably enhance the value of the landed property in the Vicinity of the Port by giving more facility to the exportation of the products of the country and an encouragement to its population.

And a natural result of these advantages will be an increase of Revenue by the Port duties which will probably make ample compensation for the Expense that will be incurred.

I need not add that every step tending to the creation or improvement of Harbours in this Country must be considered as a Patriotic exertion.

Within two miles of Watchet near to Orchard Wyndham there is a good quarry of Grit & Stone very proper for the face of the Pier. There is plenty of Rubble, Stone and some good for front stone on the coast near the Spot and the best Lime in the World for Building in Water is found there in plenty, to burn which it will be adviseable to erect Lime Kilns near the Place, the Sand is not of the best Quality but by washing such of it as may be wanted for front mortar, it will do very well.

With these Materials a Pier conformable to the Place and Section the length about 460 feet the mean height 20 feet exclusive of the Parapet, the breadth or thickness at the base 20 feet and the breadth at the top 12 feet should not exceed in Expense the Estimate annexed.

The present Pier and the Walls lining the Harbour are more indebted for their continuance to the natural goodness of the cement than to judicious construction but the late repairs and what are now underhand and very properly managed, the new Pier will lend greatly to the presentation of the old Works by the Shelter it will give to them.

15

	£		
Preparing the Foundation	100	0	0
24000, Superficial feet of Ashlar at 1/3d	1500	0	0
4760 Cubic Yds of Rubble Masonry in the Body			
of the Pier at 6 Sh per Yard	1426	0	0
Paving the Top of the Pier 420 sq. Yds at 6d	126		
Contingencies at £10 per Cent	315		
	£3467		

I am your Lordships

Very humble Servant,

Newark July 27/97   W. Jessop

Why the Earl of Egremont did not build the new East Pier as advised by William Jessop is not clear, but in 1806 Jessop's advice was again sought by Estate steward Henry Tripp for an alternative scheme. This was for a single row of piles which would obviously cost much less than the proposed new East Pier.

Surprisingly Jessop agreed that the row of piles would give a considerable degree of protection but suggested the piles be braced from the inside to prevent them being shaken loose by the heavy seas and to be "set not more than one foot asunder." The piles were erected in 1807/8 at a cost of £1356-19-11. In 1809 William Boswell was appointed Water Bailiff (the old name for Harbour Master).

By 1811 it was obvious that the row of piles was not giving much shelter to shipping in the harbour. The Shipowners and Merchants at this time favoured a new plan for the construction of an enclosed floating dock, they therefore compiled and sent a most appealing letter to the Earl of Egremont, to provide the wherewithall to build it.

To the Right Honorable George Earl of Egremont

Baron Cockermouth

My Lord,

We the undersigned Merchants and principal inhabitants of the Port of Watchet, having maturely considered the disadvantages to which the Trade of this place is exposed, and being sensibly assured of the facility, which presents for its improvement and extension, do most humbly and respectfully solicit Your Lordships kind protection towards restoring this once

Famous Engineer, William Jessop, who built Bristol's floating harbour and
advised improvement of Watchet harbour in 1797 — Photograph from the
book "William Jessop, Engineer."

(By courtesy Charles Hadfield, co-author)

respectable (Borough) Town to the advantages which nature so conspicuously points out.

My Lord — the present great expense well as risque, incurred by Vessels lying in the Harbour as it now is principally on account of hard ground and exposure are facts, we all most readily agree in and sorely lament, nor can we point other remedy out, than by the construction of an Inner Harbour.

My Lord — we presume from the present state of our local condition, to offer our best conviction for its utility and success through an undertaking neither tedious or expensive but having already expressed ourselves to Mr Tripp on this behalf we deem it more respectful to avoid particulars, doubting not but the condescention of that Gentleman (whose kind attention to our welfare we gratefully acknowledge) will state to Your Lordship, every consideration, upon which we so anxiously look for turning the propriety of our object.

My Lord — we trust you will not feel displeasure at the freedom we take in thus addressing you, for Born as the most of us are, and our ancestry also under the mild and fostering influence of Your Lordship's illustrious race! We hail the name of Wyndham, dear to us! and as plain honest Englishmen, who knowing better how to associate than to express their gratitude, we bow obedience to Your Lordship's pleasure, most sincerely praying that Health, Happiness and prosperity (three of the greatest blessings which this world can bestow) may long and very long intwine with the Honors of Your Noble House.

And with the most profound respect
We remain
My Lord
Your Lordships

Watchet

22nd November 1811

very faithfully attached

Humble Servants

Mich'l Winter	Francis Jenkins
Rich'd Whaddon	Th Thorne
William Hole	William Potter
W Basley	Robert Potter
Nicholas Tanner	William Gimblett
John Date	Thomas Whaddon
George Royal	John Bryan
George Hole	Thos Burton
Cornelias Woodland	Rich Grimes

Shortly after this Josias Jessop (the son of William Jessop) met the Earl and in March 1812 estimated the expense of making a Floating Dock at Watchet at £7446-10-0. Another letter to the Earl in April 1812 from Henry Tripp also pointed out the advantages of a new sheltered floating dock as compared with the existing unsheltered harbour. The Earl however did not respond as was hoped and no dock was built.

The writer possesses a photostat copy of what is believed to be the outline tracing of Josias Jessop's proposed floating dock. It is interesting to note that had the proposed dock been constructed it would have entailed the demolition of The Old Mill, The London Inn and several cottages including No. 6 the one at which the writer today resides *(See overleaf)*.

Another famous man to visit Watchet was J. W. Turner — the renowned painter of seascapes. He made a sketch of the harbour in 1811 from the high cliffs on the eastern side. It depicts the old pier which had been built by Sir William Wyndham in 1708 and also shows the crude breakwater of tree trunks or row of piles which had been erected in 1807 by Henry Tripp and which were intended to give some shelter in the harbour from the easterly winds. A few small vessels are shown in the harbour and on the cliff top lengths of woollen cloth have been laid out to dry, fishermen can be seen laying out nets on the beach, a very tranquil scene of the harbour which was soon to be interrupted by the Industrial Revolution *(See overleaf)*.

Cargoes of timber were shipped from Watchet for the Navy in the early 1800s. Good Somerset elm and ash was in demand for the massive wooden fighting ships built at that time. A poster dated 1816 gave notice of a forthcoming Auction Sale at the George Inn at Watchet. 108 Capital Maiden Elm Trees adapted for Navy purposes with their Tops & Lops as well as 28 Ash and one Beech Tree were to be auctioned as standing in the parishes of St. Decuman's Old Cleeve and Brompton Ralph.

The location of the aforementioned George Inn at Watchet is not known by the writer but the whereabouts of another old and long forgotten pub with a much more interesting and tempting name was situated in Market St. (Now Nos 11 & 12). It was "The Sailors Delight" and in 1841 the landlady was Anne Bryce.

The Bethel Flag 1823

Sailors' Friendly Societies of a religious character flourished at large seaports such as Bristol and attracted new members from visiting sailors including some from the small ports such as Watchet. One of these societies or Missions known as the "Brotherhood of the Sea" started a new branch of the Brotherhood at Watchet. In 1823 a Watchet sea captain having obtained an authentic "Brotherhood of the Sea" flag bearing the word "Bethel" in large letters hoisted it to the masthead of his ship in the Harbour as signal for Divine Service. Encouraged by the response the Bethel flag was then taken to Minehead, and hoisted to the masthead of the ship *Fair Trader*. This greatly upset Mr. Searle and Mr. Warren the local Customs Collectors who warned the sailors that they were liable to a fine of £500 for hoisting an *unauthorised flag* either at Minehead or Watchet.

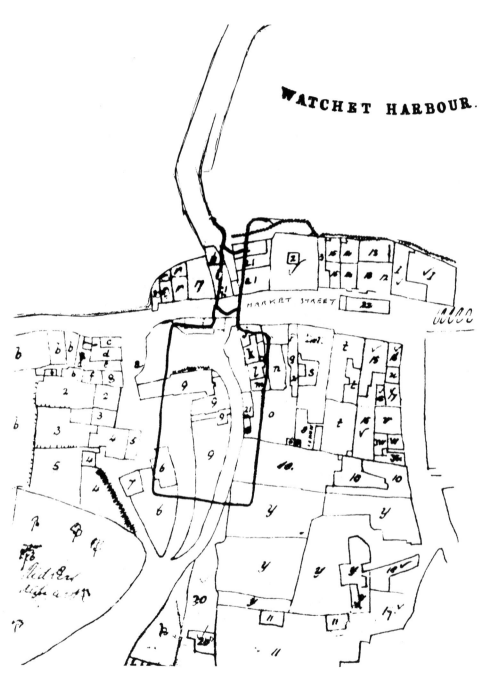

Outline of proposed floating harbour at Watchet as suggested by the engineer, Josias Jessop in 1812.   *(By courtesy of the Wyndham family)*

Engraving of a sketch of Watchet harbour by J. M. W. Turner, R.A. (1811)

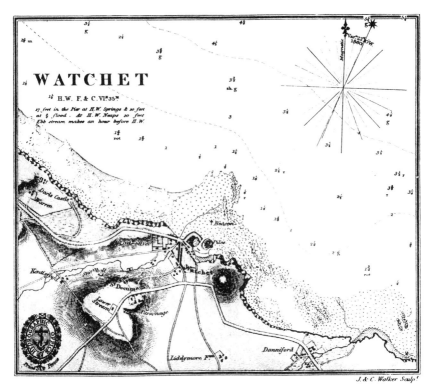

A chart of Watchet harbour. Surveyed by Lt. Denham, R.N., 1832.
(By courtesy Hydrographic Dept., Taunton)

Returning to Watchet and by this time getting their dander up, they again hoisted the Bethel Flag aboard Captain William Gimblett's ship the Sociable Friends, sure enough down rushed the Customs officials full of wind and self importance insisting the flag be lowered immediately, or else etc. What Captain Gimblett said to the Customs officials is unfortunately not recorded, but the dispute eventually got sorted out after the sailors had written to Lord Gambier, the President of the British and Foreign Seamen's Friendly Society in London. Lord Gambier went to the Commissioners of Customs about the matter and they gave orders to the Minehead and Watchet Customs officers to refrain from interference in religious matters.

Another interesting aspect of Watchet's harbour, is provided by a chart which was surveyed by Lt. Denham R.N. in 1832.

Outside of the little harbour is shown a Beacon. This would have been in the form of a tall post which besides marking the fairway would have been used to haul sailing vessels out of the harbour when contrary or lack of winds prevented them sailing out.

The old Saxon Hill Fort on the cliff top is referred to as Darls Castle (not

Daws Castle). Also revealed is the existence and route of several roads or tracks which have long since disappeared.

In 1834 the Port of Minehead was downgraded and henceforth all Minehead and Watchet ships were to be registered at Bridgwater.

It is thought that both Minehead and Watchet harbours were at this time allowed Legal Quay status which permitted the import or export of a considerable number of very varied commodities.

(Watchet's *Legal Quay* status will be referred to later.)

The unauthorised flag.

CHAPTER 3

1835-1864

WATCHET OVERTAKEN BY THE INDUSTRIAL REVOLUTION

According to a paragraph in the Taunton Courier in 1835 Iron was mentioned as one of the commodities carried by Watchet ships to South Wales. In 1837 George O'Brien Wyndham, the 3rd Earl of Egremont, was succeeded by George Francis Wyndham, the 4th Earl of Egremont, who now controlled the harbour.

By 1838 he was aware of the increasing demand for iron ore by the Smelting Works in Wales and of deposits of ore in the nearby Brendon Hills. With this in mind he commissioned George Rennie another eminent engineer at that time to plan and estimate the cost of enlarging the harbour and also building a floating dock complete with lock gates. Rennie's first estimate for the work was £11,975. This was increased after some correspondence with the Earl to £15,026. A letter from Engineer Rennie to the Earl which accompanied the second estimate ended with the words: "70 per cent for iron ore is enormous which generally speaking yields about 30 per cent."

Like his predecessor, the 4th Earl held back and no enlarged or floating harbour was constructed.

More Smuggling

The Watchet sloop *Prudence and Ann,* John Lukey master, was condemned for illicit trading and broken up at Fowey in 1835.

A notable seizure was made by night in St. Audries Bay near Watchet. In 1841, a Riding Officer surprised the crew of the Falmouth sloop *Kitty & Clara* in the act of unloading tubs. He, singlehanded, captured the vessel and her crew of three and 383 gallons of brandy and geneva (gin) valued at £50. The ship was offered for sale at a local auction but failed to find a buyer and was cut up and sold for firewood.

In 1851 nine casks were seized as they drifted ashore near Quantoxhead. A few days later another cask was found in a hedgerow half empty, a misguided bibulant was found dead nearby.

Renovations to old properties near the harbour in recent years have uncovered hiding places obviously used by smugglers, and many people believe in the existence of a smugglers tunnel linking certain premises in Market Street.

24

Three for squire and one for parson

By 1843, constant erosion by the sea was threatening to undermine valuable property near the harbour, most of which belonged to the Fourth Earl of Egremont and he decided therefore to build a new sea wall, which after much infilling formed what is now known as the Esplanade. A number of cottages were demolished at this time to enable the Esplanade and also the town slip to be built.

The new slip was to facilitate the loading and unloading of ships, the cargoes being taken via the new slipway in horse drawn carts.

John Allen was in charge of the work using stone blasted from Miltons Rocks, situated near the low water mark at nearby Doniford. The contract was supervised by Henry Hooper of Exeter (who possibly drew up the plans). The building of the new Esplanade without doubt prevented further erosion of the Earl's property but it did not please the ships' masters and owners for the seas now rebounded from the new sea wall back into the harbour.

Conditions were therefore worse than before and caused much discontent among the sea-faring men.

In 1845 the fourth Earl died and the harbour from that time was administered by a body known as the Egremont Trustees.

George Francis Wyndham, the 4th Earl of Egremont, who built Watchet's
Esplanade in 1843.　　　　　　　　*(By courtesy of the Wyndham family)*

An interesting document among the Wyndham papers at the Somerset Record Office gives a very clear picture of the Harbour Trade in 1847.

A REPORT TO THE ADMIRALTY (Harbours & Railways Dept.)

ARRIVALS & SAILINGS AT WATCHET,
YEAR ENDING 31st DECEMBER 1847.

ARRIVALS	VESSELS	SAILINGS	VESSELS
In cargo	226	In cargo	177
In ballast	28		
Total arrivals	254	Total sailings	249

TONNAGE OF CARGO — INWARDS & OUTWARDS
COASTWISE & FOREIGN

Chief articles of import and export	Coastwise inwards, tons	Coastwise outwards, tons	Foreign inwards, tons	Foreign outwards, tons
Coal	6954			
Coffee	3			
Cotton/Wool manufactured	3			
Grain	1296	539	165	
Iron manufactured	34			
Lead	5			
Limestone	28	970		
Sugar	36			
Tea	3			
Timber	120			
Tin	2			
Wool	2			
Miscellaneous	628	1628		

MISCELLANEOUS ARTICLES CONSISTED PRINCIPALLY OF FLOUR, SALT, JUNK, TAR, PITCH, OILS, SALTFISH, HAY, BRAN, SODA, CANDLES, REED, SOAP.

VESSELS BELONGING TO THE PLACE

UNDER 50 TONS:		OVER 50 TONS:	
VESSELS	TONS	VESSELS	TONS
8	257	3	159

VESSELS	BOATS
NIL	10 Flat boats used in stake fishing

Estimated number of seamen	Estimated number of fishermen
40	20

Note: Junk = old ropes cut up to make oakum and used by shipwrights for caulking seams of vessels

A small shipbuilding industry was carried on at Watchet mainly during the early 1800s (as detailed later). It was brought to an end in 1859 by harbour development. The last ship to be built was the schooner Star of the West in 1859.

1850

As early as 1850 Richard Stoate Date an enterprising Watchet man had started to organise steamboat excursions in the Bristol Channel. He was among the first to do so. The steamers which he chartered at that time were very primitive and some had originally been built as paddle tugs. With a brass band on board they picked up passengers from the Welsh ports and Bristol and brought them to Watchet, Minehead and Ilfracombe and occasionally even to a little pleasure pier built at nearby Lilstock by Sir Peregrine Acland Hood. In 1850 one of these steamers arrived at Watchet late on tide. A brief report states that 6 persons were drowned through wanton carelessness in embarking at Watchet during a pleasure trip by the *Neath Abbey*. The names of some other ships chartered by Date were *Stevenson, Defiance, Caledonia, Petrel, Heather Belle* and *Earl of Dunraven.*

By the early 1850's the Ironmasters and Industrialists from the large smelting works situated at Ebbw Vale on the opposite side of the Bristol Channel were eagerly seeking supplies of iron ore to feed their hungry blast furnaces. To supply them, new mines were sunk on the Brendon Hills, about six miles from Watchet and in 1855 a newly formed West Somerset Mineral Railway Company started construction of a standard gauge railway track to convey the ore from the mines to the harbour. A proposal to build a simple and temporary jetty projecting 20 ft into the harbour from their own yard at the top of the slipway was opposed by some of the local ship owners and master mariners who wrote to the Egremont Trustees, the Harbour Authority at that time.

To the Trustees of the late Earl of Egremont

Gentlemen,

We the undersigned Merchants Shipowners & Masters of Vessels in the Port of Watchet, in the County of Somerset having been called upon by L. Walker Esqre one of the Trustees of the late Earl of Egremont to consider an application made by the Iron Ore Company for permission to allow the Company to place and rest on the floor of the Harbour two or four Posts as may be necessary to enable the Company to construct a Stage or Jetty extending North from their Yard from 20 to 25 feet into the Harbour to enable the Company to ship their Ore from their Yard and goods and Merchandise from Vessels to their Yard.

We believe that the Jetty or Stage fixed as proposed will be highly dangerous to the Vessels laying at the Stage as well as to all other Vessels and Cargoes lying in the Harbour at the same time for the following reasons.

1st – From the smallness and exposed state of the Harbour it is with great difficulty that the Vessels belonging to this Port can be held at their moorings.

2nd – Should a Vessel be caught laden loading or discharging at the Jetty with a strong Wind, it being the most exposed place in the Harbour, she will go adrift and do considerable damage to herself and many other Vessels by cutting their moorings – in which case they would foul each other sink or fill with water and do considerable damage to their cargoes consisting of Corn, Flour, Malt and dry Goods.

3rd – That the relative values of the Cargoes bears no comparison, inasmuch as the general Cargoes of the Trading Vessels would amount in value to from £500 to £2000 whereas a Cargo of Iron Ore if immersed in winter would sustain no damage.

4th – We therefore pray the Trustees of the late Earl of Egremont to protect our interest in this matter and prevent the erection of the proposed Jetty.

Watchet – 3rd December 1855:

William Stoate	Shipowner & Merchant
R I Gimblett	do.
John Thorn	do.
M I Gimblett	do.
Rich Case	do.
Thos Date	Late Master Mariner
John Wedlake	Shipowner & Master Mariner
George Wedlake	do.
Henry Chidgey	do.

There is no evidence that this small jetty was built.

Watchet harbour was considered too small to handle an estimated 50,000 tons of ore per annum, and at this time there was some dispute as to its

29

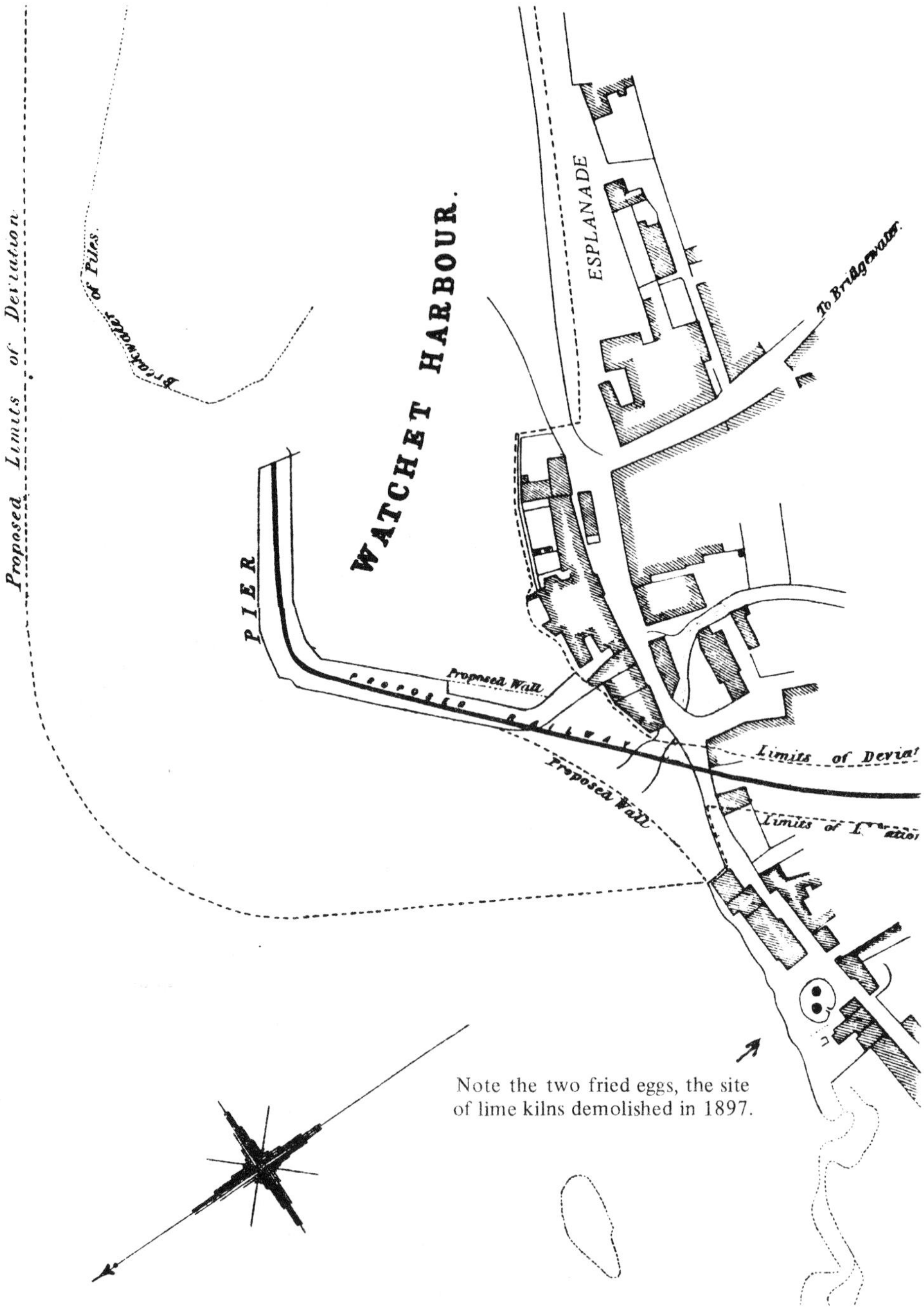

WATCHET HARBOUR.

PIER

ESPLANADE

To Bridgewater

Proposed Limits of Deviation

Breakwater of Piles

Proposed Wall

Proposed Wall

Limits of Devia'

Limits of D...atio..

Note the two fried eggs, the site
of lime kilns demolished in 1897.

Plan of the old harbour, c. 1854, showing proposed new sea wall, necessary
to give the mineral railway access to the pier over land reclaimed from the
sea.   *(Wyndham papers – Somerset Record Office)*

ownership. Previous Acts of Parliament giving authority to collect dues for various periods of time had apparently lapsed. The Admiralty sent James Abernethy (an Engineer) to report on the situation and eventually after much legal wrangling the harbour was declared to be a public one. Private capital was available and Abernethy advised the building of an enlarged harbour. Authority to take over and enlarge the harbour was eventually granted to a new consortium — mainly already shareholders in the newly formed Mineral Railway and Brendon Hills Iron Ore Company, but also including representatives from the Egremont Estate and the West Somerset Railway Co. who at this time were preparing to bring another railway to link Watchet and its Harbour with Taunton, the County Town of Somerset, also one representative from the Watchet Shipowners.

Eleven Commissioners representing these various interests in the running of the harbour were appointed in 1857. The Commissioners met at the Bell Inn on September 24th of that year and appointed Mr. Peter Boswell, the former water bailiff, as harbourmaster at a salary of £40 per annum.

The second meeting in 1857 was in the school room over the Market House. All later meetings of the Commissioners were held at the Mineral Railway Company's Offices at Station House, in Market Street.

In November 1858 Mr. Rice Hopkins, the Mineral Railway engineer who had drawn plans for an enlarged harbour, was reported to have died and Harbour Master Peter Boswell's employment was abruptly terminated. Capt. Robert Bussell of Bridgwater was appointed new harbourmaster at a salary of £20 per annum + 10% of dues.

A foretaste of what was to come in later years occured in October 1859. The Harbour Commissioners had to call a crisis meeting as a terrific storm had severely damaged the old harbour. Four ships in the harbour were completely wrecked and one vessel the *Medora* on voyage to Newport, and loaded with iron ore was lost with all hands. This particular storm in fact caused horrendous damage all around the coast of Britain. Many ships and hundreds of lives were lost including the great steam clipper *Royal Charter* 2719 tons which went ashore on the Anglesea coast with the loss of 459 people, most of whom were returning to England from Australia. This gale was afterwards always referred to as the "Royal Charter Gale".

Referring to the damaged harbour, the harbour commissioners' Minute Book sets a poser — I quote:— "the storm made a breach of upwards of 20 yards in length at the spot where the Wyndham Arms stood, washing away the parapet and the back wall and filling of the pier."

In the writer's opinion the Wyndham Arms referred to was possibly a stone plaque or monument, bearing the ornamental coat of arms of the Wyndham family and was built into the original masonry of the pier.

Repairs were put in hand, as the old pier was to remain in situ to act as a jetty. The writer also suggests that the barometer which is today situated on Watchet's Esplanade might have been provided as a result of the aforementioned storm of 1859. An identical barometer at the National Maritime Museum, (an Admiral Fitzroy *Storm* Barometer) has the following words appended: "In 1859 the British Isles were swept by a great storm causing great loss of life. In an attempt to prevent a repetition of this calamity, *Storm* Barometers were issued to Harbour communities all around the coast."

A brass plate on Watchet's barometer states that it was the gift of Sir A. A. Hood Bart. No date is visible but it has always been appreciated and made good use of by Watchet mariners and to this day is voluntarily kept clean and polished.

The Commissioners had for some time been considering various plans for enlarging the harbour. The mineral railway engineer, Rice Hopkins, had put forward a plan. James Abernethy had also produced a plan, and another had been submitted to the Egremont Trustees by the famous engineer, Isambard Kingdom Brunel. The Commissioners heard at a meeting on December 1st 1859 that Mr. Brunel had died. They had already decided on implementing Mr. Abernethy's plan but were in correspondence with Mr. Brunel concerning the same. Both Brunel and Hopkins' estimated the cost of a new harbour to be £20,000. Abernethy's estimate for a harbour built to his plan £15,250. For those interested in Watchet Harbour's history a study of the alternative plans is well worth while.

Hopkins and Abernethy both envisaged a road 30 foot wide, to be built parallel with, but on the seaward side of the Esplanade. This would link the two piers and it was also proposed that the two railway systems should eventually be linked via this route. To make this possible many houses on the North side of Market Street were to be demolished. Whereas the plans by these two engineers also proposed a river culvert to the harbour through the Mineral Yard. Brunel would have taken it by a more direct route into the corner of the harbour, near the London Inn. The plans also reveal that large lime kilns were situated at the top of the slipway at West Street and at Govier's Lane.

The land adjoining Yard beach on the Eastward side of the harbour is on Brunel's plan schedule referred to as Rack Close. The word Rack provides further evidence of and a link with the very long established Watchet woollen weaving industry. The various properties which would be affected by the proposed harbour developments are all numbered and it is interesting to look up the schedule attached to the plans which gives the names of the then current owners and occupiers. As subsequent events will show and with hindsight it can only be regretted that Brunel's plan for the new harbour was not taken up by the commissioners, instead of the cheaper and less substantial version as planned by Abernethy.

The New Harbour and Increased Trade

The construction of the new harbour to Abernethy's plan started in 1861 and was completed by 1863. From the knuckle of the old harbour a mainly

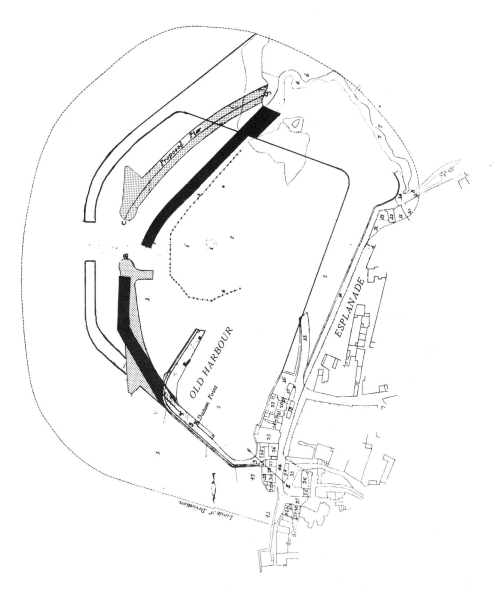

Plans to enlarge and improve the harbour were submitted by three Engineers. All three plans are shown here in juxtaposition and extending from the old harbour. The larger version submitted by Rice Hopkins is shown unshaded. The smaller plan by James Abernethy is heavily shaded and the medium size plan submitted by the famous Brunel is lightly shaded. *(Wyndham papers – Somerset Record Office)*

An early engraving of the busy harbour c.1863.

wooden breakwater was constructed; it was 390 ft in length and was equipped with an impressive cast iron lighthouse and also a signalling mast. The hexagonal cast iron tower of this lighthouse was supplied by Hennet Spink & Else of Bridgwater in 1862 and cost £75 – (it is still in service to-day).

The lantern for the top complete with oil lamp cost £90 and was supplied by Messrs. Stevens & Sons presumably of London for the cost of transporting it from London to Watchet by the newly formed Watchet Trading Co. was £2.18.5. and twelve shillings was paid to one Alfred Wedlake for assisting to erect the lantern. A composite stonework and wooden East pier 590 ft in length was also built to give protection from Easterly winds. Yard beach and the port's only shipbuilding site was enclosed and filled in to form an East Wharf.

With the construction of this wharf the Commissioners were faced with the enormous task of backfilling thousands of tons of rubble, behind its newly built wharf wall and the large area extending back to the boundary of the newly arrived West Somerset Railway linking Watchet to Taunton. They solved the problem by selling all the ground between the new harbour wall and the railway boundary to the Railway Company for the sum of £50 plus the agreement of that company to fill in behind the East Wharf and also behind the proposed new roadway which was to be built alongside the Esplanade. The Commissioners retained only 30 ft in width from the edge of the wharf, for harbour use.

34

Watchet was the terminus for the broad gauge Railway from Taunton,
hence the engine on the turntable c. 1870. Between the engine and the
harbour is the vital storage space which was sold to the Railway Company
in 1862.

This was an agreement they, and their successors, were later to bitterly
regret.

The Esplanade road was never constructed and ownership of the land
adjoining the East Wharf gave the Railway Company a stranglehold over the
future development of the harbour.

Any busy Harbour or Dock needs lots of storage space and warehouses
for cargoes. The Commissioners had relinquished the only plot of adjacent
land which was suitable for this purpose. The land was used to some extent
by the Railway Co. mainly for their own benefit. Perhaps, understandably,
they did not wish to encourage harbour trade which would compete with
their own transport of heavy goods by rail.

The new iron ore trade gave a great boost to the local shipping families.
For generations they had barely been earning a living with their little smacks
and ketches. The main trade had been bringing coal from the Welsh ports
and an occasional cargo of grain but, more often than not, they had to sail
from Watchet without an outward cargo. Now there would be plenty of
cargoes each way. More ships were required for the extra trade.

As before mentioned the shipbuilding yard had been destroyed by the
construction of the East Wharf, but some of the enterprising shipwrights
took their tools and gear to Helwell Bay about half a mile to the East of the
harbour, and, although the facilities did not allow for the building of new
vessels, they took some of the smaller smacks, hauled them high and dry
onto the beach and then literally cut them in half. After dragging the two

sections apart they built in a new middle section to give a much larger cargo carrying capacity.

The building of the East Pier had unfortunately been carried out without regard to the interests of the limekiln owners in Goviers Lane who now found their access to the foreshore for collecting limestones was only possible when the tide had left the harbour entrance. Whereas previously their pannier- ed donkeys used to walk along the beach to collect limestones one hour after high water, they now had to wait until at least three hours after high water before they could make their way down the town slip and through the harbour entrance. Other commercial users of the foreshore also complained to the Commissioners. As a result of the complaints a new slipway was built in 1863 to give access to the beach at Culver Cliff (which is now known as Splash Point).

In 1864 Thomas Langdon & William Besley were paid £39.10.0 for blast- ing rocks to form a crude roadway at the bottom of the new slipway. This was necessary to enable horses and carts to get to the fishing stake nets on the foreshore, and to collect building stones and shingle etc. The route of this old track is still visible.

The slipway can be seen in early photographs and engravings of the harbour. Being built in a most exposed position, it was washed away by storms after some years.

The new enlarged harbour built to the plan of James Abernethy. This early photograph c.1860s shows the slipway used by horse-drawn carts, and panniered donkeys to obtain limestone and building materials from the beach.

Another business which was interrupted at this time was the long established business of rope making carried out by the Besley family. This was remedied by moving it to another site at Doniford Road where it continued for many years.

Beside the new iron ore trade other businesses at Watchet increased at this time. The long standing Flour Mills situated near Anchor Street and owned by the Stoate family was modernised and made much more use of the harbour. Quite a number of vessels were engaged in bringing supplies of grain and sailing with cargoes of flour and bran etc.

The Watchet paper mill also at this time imported tons of rags for paper making from continental ports; coal was also required for the boilers of the mills and for many other small local industries as well as for domestic use and the engines of the Mineral Railway.

Many vessels leaving Watchet with ore for Newport would from there pick up a cargo of coal for Ireland. Here they might well obtain a cargo of wheat or oats for Watchet but at times they had to return in ballast. The ballast from Ireland was usually in the form of stones, and some of Watchet's terraces of houses were built with these Irish ballast stones, i.e. Portland and Almyr.

The contract for building the new harbour had been secured by Mr. William Tredwell for the sum of £15,068-10-2d. The figure seems very low in view of the massive construction and excavation work involved.

During the construction of the harbour in Feb. 1861 the Free Press reported:– "On Saturday last one of those objectionable 'strikes' alike injurious to master and men took place among the labourers employed in constructing Watchet Harbour. The men we understand want 3/- per tide – that is for about five or six hours work – the contractor appears to be paying 2s. 3d at present. Some of the men however have thought better of the affair and have returned to their work."

A later comment in the same newspaper:– "The workmen in keeping with a practice usual at the time loved to sing snatches of song during their toil. Their favourite ditty was a topical one and was said to have been composed by a rhymster at Williton. The opening lines run like this:–

> Now my lads come down this way,
> The tide is ebbing from the Quay,
> Tom Williams is gone out to Sea
> And Baker's in the harbour."

The new harbour had hardly been completed early in 1863 when defects in the structure were becoming apparent. The following report from the harbourmaster Captain Bussell to the Commissioners did not augur well for the future.

Mr Chairman

& Gentlemen

The damage occasioned by the heavy Gales of the last month to the Wall of the old Western Pier Breakwater and East Pier has now been repaired. The former at the expense of the Harbour Board, the two latter at the cost of Mr. Tredwell. The planking washed up on Breakwater has been refastened by 9 inch spikes which before was only six inch. The Plank washed away from the East Pier has been replaced and two additional ones added the whole to appearance seems secure I am pleased to be able to state no farther settlement of the Masonry of the west end of the east Pier has taken place. The old Piles advertised for sale by Tender has been bought by Mr. Thorne at 4d per cube foot there being no higher tenders.

This being your first meeting for 1863 I beg to lay before you the trade of your port for the past and two preceding years.

	No. of vessels inwards	Gross Revenue
1860	486	£466- 0-0
1861	524	£530- 0-0
1862	557	£688-16-0

I am Gents, yours faithfully,
Robt. Bussell.

In 1864 Captain Bussell obviously apprehensive as to possible storm damage to his new harbour wrote to the Commissioners and his letter as follows indicates that he was on the ball.

Watchet Harbour Office,
Sept 12 1864

Mr Chairman

& Gentlemen

Very high Spring Tides approaching together with the Sun crossing the Equator give me reasons for expecting heavy Equinoctal Gales.

I have had during the past week the Wall of the old West Pier carefully examined and all defects appearing stopped with Cement by Masons under Jonathan Chedgey.

I hope the Board will today examine the slip and damaged baulk on the East Pier and give instructions for the same to be repaired.

I am Gents, yours faithfully,
Robt. Bussell.

CHAPTER 4

1864-1899
THE HEYDAY, THEN SLOW DECLINE OF HARBOUR TRADE

New Ships

New and larger ships were required to deal with the increased volume of harbour trade. The *Star of the West* had been especially built for the new trade at Watchet in 1859 by the shipwright George Escott Geen.

The Besley family bought the new *Kelso* from far away Prince Edward Island near Nova Scotia in 1868.

The Stoate family who owned the rapidly expanding flour mills ordered the *Express* to be built at Swansea in 1861. She was followed by the *Telegraph* from Westacott's yard at Barnstaple in 1869 and the *Electric* which was also built by Westacott's in 1871.

The Allen family had the *Heather Bell* built especially strongly for the iron ore trade as the heavy cargo tended to strain vessels which were loaded while lying aground. She was built by Westacott's in 1870.

The Allens also had the *Dashwoods* built at Bridgwater in 1878 by John Gough.

Many other schooners, ketches and smacks were bought and run as business ventures by local families of modest means who might own part or the whole of the 64 shares in each vessel. The total shares in each vessel by long established practice always numbered 64.

Shipwrights, sailmakers, ropemakers, blockmakers and coopers all found extra work, as well as the workers in the small iron and brass foundries.

Practically everything that was required aboard ship was made in the town. Everyone had a job and the harbour was a hive of activity.

The Mineral Railway brought thousands of tons of iron ore from the Brendon Hill mines to the newly erected Hydraulic tips on the West Pier jetty.

The thunderous noise as truckloads of ore cascaded down shutes into the ships' holds, went on from dawn to dusk.

Old people have recalled that at weekends, trainloads of miners from the Brendon Hill Iron Ore Mines came into town for a night out. The pubs did a roaring trade. At times fists flew as drunken miners came into contact with equally drunken foreign and local sailors who were ashore at the time. Watchet on occasion resembled a town from the Wild West and was indeed a boom town.

39

This interesting photograph c. 1870s shows 17 ships in port. One on each side of the iron ore jetty (top centre), are loading under the hydraulic tips. On the East Wharf (left centre), a cart is about to be loaded from the ship below by a horse operated crane. Piles of tree trunks on the Railway-owned foreground are about to be sawn into baulks or planks, probably for use on the broad gauge railway, or for harbour repairs. Note the ladder protruding from the sawpit (front left).

A large brig the "Emma Ernest" in port, another has just left under tow by a tug. On edge of quay can be seen a wooden shute used for loading ships with sacks of flour, bran, etc. c. 1880's.

(By courtesy Michael Bouquet)

An occasional cargo of wheat would be brought in Continental ships for use in Watchet's Flour Mills which explains the reason for this Dutch Schooner being moored in the harbour. Note the unusual square windows in her stern. The large chimney stack behind the tall building on the right served Watchet's Iron Foundry.   *(By courtesy Michael Bouquet)*

Photograph shows the hydraulic tips on the iron ore jetty, 1870s. In the foreground a steam ship probably the Saint Decumans was one of two wooden steam ships built at Bridgwater.

Harbour master Bussell died in 1867 and Mr Edwin Forde was appointed in May of that year.

Considerable gale damage to the West Pier and East Pier slip in 1869 proved very costly and Engineer Abernethy advised the erection of two groynes at the West Pier.

Thomas Griffiths, who had provided a steam crane on the East Pier in 1870, requested that a water supply be made available.

By the year 1872 there were 37 ships registered as belonging to or trading from the harbour of Watchet as follows:

NAME OF VESSEL	Reg. Tonnage	REGISTERED OWNERS
Thomas & Sarah	36	Allen John
Helen	59	Allen John
Heather Bell	52	Allen John
Fortitude	40	Allen John
Taunton	52	Allen Robert
Kelso	67	Besley William & Besley John
Lloyds	24	Browning Eliza & Wedlake Robert
Love	42	Bryant George
Charles Phillips	31	Case Richard Date
Star of the West	81	Cox Samuel & Taylor George
Martha	81	Davis Thomas Martin
Providence	78	Griffiths Thomas
Minerva	63	Griffiths Thomas
Sisters	81	Griffiths Thomas
Staunch	71	Goodland Thomas & Goodland Charles
Ocean	48	Hole Charles
Friendship	67	Hole William Henry Perkins
Thomasine & Mary	48	Hole Henry George
Friends (Little)	33	Hole Llewellin
John	43	Johnson William
John George	37	Kingsbury Joseph Lewis
Richard	37	Norman John
Tartar	40	Nicholas John Henry
Ann	54	Passmore George
Chrystal Bell	94	Passmore George
Taunton Packet	82	Press Henry
Gannet	46	Prosser William
Mary Lauder	36	Prosser William
Laurina	17	Skinner James
Electric	45	Stoate William
Express	45	Stoate William
Hawk	59	Stoate William

NAME OF VESSEL	Reg. Tonnage	REGISTERED OWNERS
Telegraph	40	Stoate William
Tom	23	Thorne John
Abeona	19	Wedlake Robert
Ceres	37	Williams Robert
Friends	46	Thorne John & Ridler John

Another steam crane was provided by H. G. Hole in 1873; his proposed charges for its use were 5½d per ton.

During the same year sheds were erected over the hydraulic tips on the iron ore jetty to protect the operators from the weather.

Although the iron ore trade was increasing and cargoes for the flour and paper mills were quite frequent, the Commissioners felt that other trade on the Eastern side of the harbour was being held back by the exorbitant charges of the West Somerset Railway Company, whose sidings served that side of the harbour. A strong protest was sent to the Railway Company on that score.

This remarkably clear photograph shows two smacks moored in the "Cot of the Quay" for repair and painting etc. Their running bowsprits have been taken inboard to avoid damage. Two schooners are laying beside the iron ore jetty, and in the middle of the harbour a schooner and a ketch are being unloaded into horse-drawn carts, one of which can be seen waiting its turn under the bowsprit of the schooner. The nearest vessel has been identified as the smack "Pioneer," Alfred Binding, master and owner. Second from the left is the schooner "Forest Deer," Steven Allen owner, Captain Bray, master.

Production of iron ore peaked in 1877 when nearly 50,000 tons were mined, but unfortunately within a few years it was to decline.

Estimates for repairs and storm damage on the West Pier and to the East Quay loading bay in 1883 totalled £1,100. The Commissioners experienced difficulty at this time in raising a loan for this work from Stuckey's Bank. But even worse news was to follow.

All mining for iron ore ceased in 1883. The Brendon Hill iron ore deposits had always proved difficult and expensive to produce, and it was now found that iron ore from Spain could be shipped to the Welsh smelting works cheaper than supplies shipped from Watchet.

The sudden loss of trade at this time was a bitter blow for Watchet and also the surrounding district, for hundreds of miners and many other people depended on the mining industry and were suddenly out of a job.

Eventually, with some difficulty, funds were raised by the Commissioners in 1884, to repair the West Pier and East Quay loading bay. But henceforth the same old story, of ever recurring gale damage was to repeat itself every few years.

After constant requests by shipowners (first mooted in 1870) and their promise to pay extra harbour dues, an extension was built at the head of the West Breakwater in 1887. The shipowners considered it would "prevent heavy seas from constantly heaving into the harbour".

The crude extension to the West Pier built in 1887 can be seen in this photograph. A regatta is taking place, hence the display of bunting.

44

The grid iron built in 1896 to enable repair to the undersides of vessels.

A Duplex anchor lantern with a red lens was set up on the new structure in 1890, but shortly afterwards it was knocked into the sea by the local smack, *Fortitude.*

Mary Allen, owner of the guilty smack, refused to pay £4.00 to replace the lantern, claiming it was an Act of God. Taken to court, she had to pay four pounds, seven shillings and sixpence.

In 1895 W. L. Copp (one of the Commissioners) and others submitted a plan and section of a *Dry Dock* to be erected on the inside of the East Pier. It was hoped this would have enabled small ships to be built and repaired.

Permission to build the dock was given, but shortly afterwards the project was abandoned, and a more modest plan was submitted and passed to provide a *Grid-iron* alongside the West breakwater.

The Grid-iron, a row of cross beams, was set on the bed of the harbour in 1896, and enabled ships' bottoms to be repaired.

It was realised at this time that Watchet's heyday was over, and no more money was invested in building new ships. Some of the best ships were sold and some of the older ones broken up. But a fair number of the fine fleet which had been built up went coasting, i.e. seeking cargoes anywhere around the coast of Britain or from the Continental ports. Cargoes of coal from the Welsh ports could usually be picked up as well as China Clay from Cornish harbours. Some Watchet ships were not seen for several years at their home port. Only at Christmas would seamen make a special effort to bring their ships back, usually with a Christmas tree hoisted to the mast-head.

45

Sometimes in their eagerness to get home for Christmas they would set sail in adverse weather conditions, and consequently on some occasions vessels and men were lost at Christmas time, causing great sorrow in the community.

Although with the loss of the iron ore trade the port had lost its main business, other industrial concerns such as the flour and paper mills continued to ship cargoes through the harbour. Consignments of locally grown timber from Messrs. Thorne's Steam Saw Mills, situated at The Cross, were also shipped away. All the districts' supplies of coal, road stone, building bricks, paraffin, groceries and furniture were at this time brought in by small sailing vessels owned and manned by local families.

A schooner dries her sails beside the wooden breakwater c. 1890's. Note the black ball hoisted on the signal mast which indicates to approaching ships that there is sufficient depth of water for them to enter harbour.

CHAPTER 5

1899-1935
THE 1900 STORM DISASTER,
AND WATCHET'S STRUGGLE FOR SURVIVAL

The Disaster

The Harbour Commissioners and shareholders who had subscribed thousands of pounds to build the new harbour got hardly any return on their capital.

Almost every other year storms would cause damage to the fabric of the harbour and with dwindling trade the necessary expensive repairs were sometimes delayed. So it was that in the year 1899 urgent repairs were required to the West Breakwater. Tenders for the work were submitted by two local contractors, Messrs. Morse, & Messrs. Greenslade in the sum of £362 and £350 respectively. These tenders were considered by the Commissioners to be too high and could therefore not be entertained. The work was postponed and orders were given to get it done by direct labour. Whether subsequent events would have been different if these repairs had been immediately carried out by the Contractors, it is impossible to say but in Dec. 1900 Disaster struck Watchet Harbour, and the story of this was vividly described at the time by journalist Will Lee in the West Somerset Free Press and later by Jack Hurley the well-known newspaper man and author.

"On Thursday 28 Dec 1900 there were unmistakeable signs of the approach of dirty weather, rain squalls, an angry moon and a strong wind veering more and more from the South West to the Westward. In anticipation local owners made their craft as snug as possible, especially so as there were, as is usual at Christmas Time a fair number of ships in port. In all they numbered thirteen.

The next morning with the approach of daylight it became apparent that the gale was increasing in fury. Out in the Channel a horrendous sea was running and the incoming tide was a scene of tremendous grandeur, the waves running to a great height. Doubts had previously been expressed as to the stability of the breakwater which had been much damaged of late. Not long after the tide had reached half flood, the structure commenced to give way under the pressure of the enormous waves, which fairly buried it and the adjoining pier at times completely hiding them from view.

Occasional glimpses were afforded of the destruction being wrought and in a comparatively short time only a baulk or so could be seen standing of

47

the straight portion of the Western breakwater. The breach proved disastrous as it allowed the sea to have full play against the shipping on the eastward side of the harbour, without giving the owners any chance of saving their property. With nothing to check the sea all the craft soon began to get into trouble and by the time high water was reached, two vessels had foundered.

To add to the difficulties of the situation three of the four vessels moored at the western end of the harbour broke adrift and drifted down against the craft at the East Wharf and pier. Here they lay grinding against each other while masts went by the board, bulwarks were stove in like matchwood, sails and gear torn to ribbons. In neither case was it possible to avert disaster.

Four men at great peril to their lives were lowered into a small boat with a view to arresting the drifting craft from the Western side of the harbour. The task was beyond them and it was only with extreme difficulty that they were taken out of the near sunken boat with ropes.

Mature and tough seamen could be seen on the quay openly weeping as they helplessly watched and heard their beloved ships grinding and groaning in agony as they ripped and tore each other to pieces. These tormented vessels represented the entire life savings of the seamen and their families and were their only means of livelihood.

Of the thirteen craft in port only three escaped the general destruction, viz. the *Electric, Forest Deer,* and the *Commodore,* the others were driven and battered about at will, words failing to give an adequate description of the havoc being wrought. When the gales eventually subsided on Saturday, the task of trying to separate the tangled mass of wrecked ships got under way.

The harbour master Capt. Watts set several boats' crews to work to bring ashore any large baulks and spars and a team of horses was engaged to drag them up the slipway into Market Street and onto the Esplanade.

Four vessels, the *Telegraph, Mary Louisa, Aurora* and *Echo* narrowly escaped sharing the fate of the craft in port, having left the harbour only the previous day. The most serious result of the gale was the loss of the breakwater as it rendered the harbour virtually untenable for shipping.

Possibly due to shock, hardly any mention of the disastrous gale damage is mentioned in the Harbour Commissioners' Minute Book, but in March 1901 the Commissioners requested Cuthbert A. Brereton, the engineer at that time of a new sea wall being constructed at nearby Blue Anchor, to inspect the damaged harbour and report.

After inspection, Brereton reported and estimated that reconstruction of the West Breakwater would cost £15,000 and suggested that a floating dock could also be built for an extra £10,000.

In April 1901 the Minute Book ended with these words:— "It was considered that the work suggested was not such as the Commissioners could carry out for want of means, and that the suggested schemes were therefore not possible."

After the howling gales and angry seas of 1900 had subsided the New Year

The disastrous gale-damaged harbour in December 1900, showing the huge breach in the West breakwater and the damaged East pier and iron ore jetty.   (By courtesy R. T. Sellick)

Some of the tangled wreckage of the ships.

broke on the little town that had lost its living. Sadly the battered remnants of the once proud fleet were put up for auction. The *Hematite,* a once smart schooner of 100 tons which now had a broken back sold for a mere £5, and the total for all that was salvaged including huge baulks of timber from the breakwater was a pathetic £200. The remains of one unsold ship, the *George May,* were offered free to anyone who would cart it away.

An atmosphere of gloom lay over the town, broken only by the tap of the auctioneer's hammer. The Commissioners and shareholders of the harbour, having already lost thousands of pounds, were understandably quite unwilling to rebuild the severely damaged harbour and risk losing even more money.

The port of a thousand years had sustained damage many times before, and had received helpful donations from many and varied sources. But it soon became clear that this time insufficient help was forthcoming. The Lord Mayor of London was asked to start a Mansion House Fund but declined.

In February a committee of principal men of the town launched an appeal that represented to the neighbourhood and county Watchet's pitiable condition consequent upon the harbour disaster. £371.14.10 was subscribed and distributed.

The major industries of the town depended on the harbour, and a large number of people were still employed in sailing or servicing ships.

The paper mills needed to import their coal and much paper was sent away by ship. Messrs. Stoates' flour mills were still expanding and made good use of the port. Something had to be done or the towns industries would die. A generous gift of 200 Elm trees by the Wyndham Estate enabled the huge gap in the Western Breakwater to be temporarily filled and the townsfolk began to take heart. At this time Watchet with nearby Williton formed the Parish of St Decumans, each electing its own representatives to serve on the same Parish Council. Watchet's townsfolk were desperately anxious to get the harbour rebuilt to ensure their future employment. It became clear to them then that no financial backing could be expected from any quarter and that they stood alone. There was only one answer to their problem. This was to form their own local authority which would enable them to borrow money on the security of the rates and thus enable them to rebuild the harbour. So it came about that in 1902 Watchet Urban District Council was formed in order to take over the authority and ownership of the harbour and thus ensure the livelihood of the majority of the townsfolk. With a population of under 2,000 it was probably the smallest Urban District Authority in the country.

1902-1911

On April 15th 1902 the first Watchet Urban District Council met at the Castle Hall in Swain Street and twelve newly elected councillors sat down to try to solve the town's problems big and small. Most of these are briefly recorded in successive Minute Books and provide some of the background of

Photograph c. 1901 shows the temporary filling of the breach in the West breakwater with 200 elm trees. A ketch is leaving harbour having been attended by a boat-load of hobblers, the returning hobble boat can be seen in the harbour entrance.

this book. Perhaps the first council, having the heavy problem of the damaged harbour to worry about, was not in a mood to deal with more mundane things. For, at its very first meeting, it decided that a letter of complaint from a Mr. Hosegood on river pollution should lie on the table.

In July 1902 Mr. W. T. Douglas was asked to act as Engineer for the harbour restoration works and in October the tender of C. H. Walker for harbour restoration amounting to £16,183-3-5 was accepted. The rateable value of the whole town at this time was £5,800.

The officers and staff of the first Council were as follows:—

Mr. Frank Risdon (Solicitor)   Town Clerk (Part time)
Mr. Willie Lee   Rate Collector (Part time)
Dr. Linden   Medical Officer of Health (Part time)
Mr. Gowen Hunt   Highway Surveyor, Sanitary Surveyor, and
    Inspector of Nuisances (Full time)
Captain Watts   Harbour Master (Full time)
Mr. Charlie Sully   Harbour Signalman (Part time)
+ 2 general labourers   Full time.

The Western breakwater was rebuilt of masonry and large concrete blocks (approx. 5 ft. square). These blocks were pre-cast in the adjacent mineral

51

yard using aggregate of fine shingle hauled by horse and cart from Doniford Beach. The old 1862 lighthouse due to a careless oversight had to be re-purchased from the firm who had the contract to demolish the old wooden breakwater. The gas lamp in the lighthouse was at this time improved, and fitted with new clockwork occulting mechanism supplied by Chance Bros & Co. of Birmingham.

The red flashing tidal light was claimed to be visible for 10 miles. A new signal mast was also set up at the head of the new breakwater.

The old iron ore jetty which was part of the original harbour of 1708 was in a state of collapse and was therefore demolished. The outer part of the East pier was turned at an angle inward and rebuilt as a wooden structure.

Hardly had the work been completed in 1903 when as if to spit in Watchet's eye, Mother Nature sent another terrible gale causing a huge breach in the East Wharf. This necessitated a further loan of £6000 to enable it to be rebuilt. During this gale the smack *Echo* was blown right out of the harbour. She drove ashore and was wrecked at East Quantoxhead amazingly at the exact spot where she often lay aground, while loading cargoes of lime stone. The ketch *Electric* which was owned by Messrs. Stoates and partly laden with flour, was sunk and wrecked by the collapse of the wharf. In 1903 Harbourmaster Watts was succeeded by Capt. Alfred Norman.

It had always been the custom at Watchet harbour that the first ship to enter the harbour on each tide would be the first to go to the unloading berth. Quite often several ships would be waiting outside the harbour for the

Further gale damage to the harbour in 1903.

52

This photograph c. 1903 shows on the left the Western breakwater newly rebuilt in masonry. The 1862 lighthouse which had survived the 1900 storm has yet to be re-erected at its head. The outer part of the opposite pier is shown being rebuilt as a wooden structure.

The newly constructed harbour c. 1905.   *(By courtesy V. Stone)*

53

tide to rise sufficiently for them to enter. A black ball raised on a signal mast would indicate to them that there was eight foot of water at the Pier Head.

During darkness the pierhead lighthouse would be lit to indicate the same state of tide. Vessels drawing eight ft or less would then race each other into the harbour. Although quite spectacular and exciting for onlookers ashore, this sometimes had disastrous results for collisions occurred and ships and piers were on occasion severely damaged.

Masters of ships drawing over eight ft obviously had to wait longer before they would have enough water to sail in, and as sometimes they had been waiting at anchor for hours longer than the shallow draught vessels, they were very unhappy at the situation.

The Council therefore in Oct. 1903 issued a notice to all ship owners and masters of ships bound for Watchet:

> 'That the first vessel that is in the proper anchorage in Blue Anchor Bay shall be the first vessel in stem for discharging' (i.e. first in turn).
>
> This order considerably reduced the number of pierhead collisions.

Dredging of the harbour was carried out in 1905 by Mr Bosley at a cost of £410. In the same year the council resolved that an Official Harbourmaster's cap complete with gold braid should be obtained for use by the Harbourmaster Captain Alfred Norman.

Coastguards were given permission in 1907 to put their boats on the Esplanade and in June of that year great excitement was stimulated by strong rumours of harbour trade revival.

Mr. H. Blomfield Smith had requested permission to take a railway locomotive across the Esplanade. H. Blomfield Smith was one of the engineers who had been involved in rebuilding the harbour. He and others had become interested in re-opening the long closed iron ore mines and in getting the industry going again. The locomotive referred to was to be used on the old mineral railway to haul the iron ore to the harbour. In due course it was transferred onto the Mineral Railway at nearby Kentsford. There were great rejoicings at the prospect of the iron ore industry being revived.

The old railway from the mines was still in situ, but the loading jetty had been demolished after the great storm of 1900. In 1908 a few shiploads of ore were again shipped from the West pier. They were tipped into the vessel's holds down a make-shift wooden shute. This was not very satisfactory and Blomfield Smith and his associates who were by this time known as the Somerset Mineral Syndicate, were permitted to erect a new wooden jetty to replace the one that had been demolished. The new jetty was 240ft long and cost £1,500. The Syndicate had very little capital and, at this time, a slump in the steel trade meant there was hardly any demand for iron ore. In June 1910 the Syndicate went into liquidation. The jetty was eventually purchased by the Council for £70 in 1911.

In Aug 1911 the Council called an emergency meeting as the port's major shipowners were to cease trading at Watchet. Messrs. Stoates' Flour Mills which had been established at Watchet for generations, had been destroyed by fire and the proprietors had decided not to rebuild the mills at Watchet but to move the entire business to newly erected premises at Bristol.

At a stroke the Council had now lost a major payer of harbour dues and rates, and a major employer of labour. To the small town, now saddled with huge repayments of harbour loans, this was indeed a bitter blow and caused considerable anxiety. Drastic cuts in expenditure had to be made. The harbour signalman, Mr. Charlie Sully, who lit and extinguished the gas lit lighthouse at the various tide times of the night and who hoisted and lowered the black signal ball also at varying tide times during the day, was given notice. The lady cleaner of the shelter and bandstand toilets etc. on the Esplanade was dismissed and one of the only two full-time labourers employed by the Council was also given the sack. All street lighting was in future to be extinguished at 10p.m. Capt. Alfred Norman, the harbour master, was told to take on all the duties of the signalman at no extra pay. This was too much to bear for Capt. Norman who, after a short while, handed in his notice.

By Dec 1911 a Solution to the Crisis was found when the Council's surveyor, Mr. Gowen Hunt, agreed to take on the extra work of Harbourmaster at no extra pay except for £10 per annum for collecting harbour dues. Mr. Charles Sully was reappointed signalman and also berthing master at a salary of only £25 per annum. Mr. Hunt carried on the many and varied

Fire at Stoate's Flour Mills, 1911. One of Watchet's main industries at that time.

duties of Harbourmaster, Surveyor and Sanitary Inspector for many years. In addition he also planned and supervised several large road widening schemes and major harbour repairs. He did literally everything and always appeared calm and unflappable. A truly remarkable man.

1911-1923

Fortunately for Watchet at this time its other main industry the Paper Mill was beginning to expand, and had started to import large quantities of wood pulp from Scandinavian countries. Hundreds of tons of culm (small coal) was required to feed the boilers at the mill and this was mainly fetched from Welsh ports by the Paper Co.'s own newly acquired steam ship the *Rushlight.*

In 1912 Messrs. Stoates' steam crane was taken over by Messrs. Gliddons, who at this time owned Watchets' Iron Foundry.

In 1912 few people at Watchet had ever seen an aeroplane. When it became known that M. Louis Salmet, a French aviator, was to fly a plane from Minehead to Weston Super Mare with a passenger Mr. Van Trump of Taunton, the whole town was at the sea front to see it fly by.

When about a mile off the harbour the engine of the plane failed and it crashed into the sea. A boat was immediately launched and quickly rowed to the scene of the crash. Amazingly both men were alive and little the worse for their experience.

These men rescued the pilot and passenger of an aeroplane that crashed into the sea off Watchet in 1912. (Left to right) Walter Norman, James Baker, Thomas Allen, Alfred Binding, Charles Escott, Alfred Langdon and John Binding. In the background can be seen the wooden jetty built by the Somerset Mineral Syndicate.

A Norwegian ship which was at anchor in the bay managed to salvage the plane before it sank and it was later brought into the harbour. The sailors who had carried out the rescue were given a reward of £5 by the *Daily Mail,* the sponsor of the flight.

In 1913 Messrs Quadley and Audsent presented plans for a new jetty to be constructed on the Eastern side of the harbour (nothing ever came of this.)

During the war years much Welsh coal was shipped through the harbour to relieve the pressure on the Severn Railway Tunnel; large amounts of pit props were shipped away as return cargoes, also locally made wooden packing cases for use in the Welsh tinplate and sheet steelworks.

In 1914 three sections of the Iron Ore Jetty built by the Somerset Mineral Syndicate were removed after damage by the steamer *Alder,* and eventually in 1917 the remainder of this wooden jetty was sold to W. J. Webb of Plymouth for £350.

Watchet sailors were not lacking in courage at this time, they continued to sail all around the coast and to France despite the dangers of minefields and attack by submarine.

Capt. James Lovell, master of the schooner *Charles* of Bridgwater, was taken prisoner by a German submarine which had sunk the *Charles* by gunfire killing the mate.

Another Watchet man Capt. Jack Hole was aboard two successive sailing ships which sank after attacks by enemy submarines.

A few older sailors at this time were called on to do duty as coast watchers and they daily patrolled the shore. Quite a few local sailors served in the Naval Reserve aboard P & A Campbell's fleet of paddle steamers which had been taken over by the Navy for the dangerous job of minesweeping.

During the latter part of the war a shortage of steel necessitated the taking up of the rails on the old disused Mineral Railway. Arthur Balmer and Thomas Barton Peel (a flamboyant character) were in charge of this operation and employed among others several sailors who were home on leave at the time. To get to work at the extreme end of the Mineral Line the sailors either walked or made use of an old hand-operated maintenance trolley which could be propelled along by manually pumping handles up and down.

An amusing tale has been told that on one occasion when the wind was quite strong and in the right direction George Strong, one of the sailors, fitted a boat's mast and lug sail onto the trolley. Thomas Barton Peel wearing a naval officers' hat, took command of the 'ship' and they sailed to work in fine style.

After the war trade again fell off and the Council desperately cast around for any means of increasing harbour revenue.

The Cardiff Marine Stores Co., a ship breaking concern, sought the exclusive use of the West pier and the berths alongside for ship breaking and offered the Council £90 per annum for these facilities plus £20 for each ship broken up. It was believed that quite a number of small or medium sized ships would be broken up and consequently quite a number of £20 collected, but the arrival of the first ship to be broken in 1920 was quite staggering. She turned out to be *H.M.S. Fox,* a battle cruiser of 7,000 tons. She was towed into the harbour by three tugs on a very high Spring tide and was by far the biggest ship ever to enter the harbour. It was 1923 before she was finally dealt with and another large ship was brought in for breaking.

This time it was the huge steel sailing barque *Dova Rio* of 2,000 tons. She was, like the *Fox* before her, gradually cut into small pieces which were sent away for scrap. Quite a number of men were employed in this industry but in 1925 the firm ran into financial difficulties and ceased trading at Watchet.

1923-1925

During 1922 permission to erect a warehouse on the East Wharf had been given to a newly formed syndicate of local businessmen, trading as The Watchet Shipping and Transport Co. Ltd. They owned a small steamship named the Karrier. Until 1924 this little ship traded in the Bristol Channel with general cargo. A large warehouse 100 ft long and 20 ft wide had been built by the syndicate on the very edge of the east wharf. (As mentioned before no other warehouse space was available to the harbour authority.)

On Aug 24 1924 the heavily loaded warehouse and a large section of the wharf collapsed into the harbour.

In October 1925 the Council belatedly decided to repair the breach by direct labour and another loan of £1200 had to be raised. Mr. Gowen Hunt was called upon to supervise the work which was put in hand by Mr. Joseph Chidgey, Master Mason. A little earlier the council had been presented with a field gun by the War Office. The idea being that it should be set up and displayed as a War Memorial. The gun had not been asked for, and as the town had already decided on a sportsground for its war memorial it was an unwanted embarrassment. The council therefore resolved that the gun should help fill up the breach in the East Wharf and if possible the barrel should form a bollard. It is not known by the writer if, in fact, the gun was buried in the wharf but certainly there is no bollard visible which in any way resembles the barrel of a gun.

Gunfire and Romance

In January 1925 Watchet's Council viewed with favour the news that an Army Summer Camp was to be established at nearby Doniford and soldiers would be trained to fire anti-aircraft guns from a cliff-top site. Little did they realise what was in store, for soon after Watchet's small fishing industry, which had existed for hundreds of years, was brought to an end by the restriction of access to the foreshore, and the fishing grounds off the harbour, and off Doniford.

The cruiser H.M.S. "Fox", July 1920. The largest ship ever to enter
Watchet harbour. The SS "Rushlight" and a ketch lay alongside the
East Pier. *(By courtesy V. Stone)*

The large barque "Dova Rio" awaits the shipbreaking gang at the West
Pier, c.1923. In the foreground is the ketch "Mizpah" and in the harbour
entrance is the ketch "Charlotte".

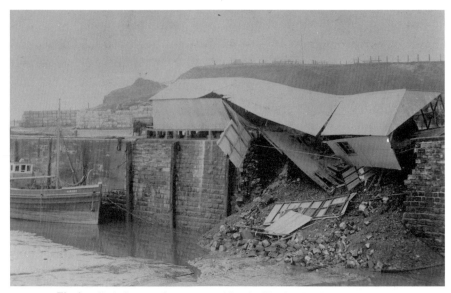

The heavily laden warehouse erected by the Watchet Trading Co. collapsed into the harbour. The Company's ship the "Karrier" seen alongside was damaged and shortly afterwards was sold – August, 1924.

Anti-Aircraft Guns at Doniford – 1930's.

In 1925 the Council wrote to support Messrs Besley's claim for compensation on this score. By 1930 the earsplitting noise from the guns had become almost unbearable. The whining noise of low flying planes constantly towing target drogues to and fro from morning until night, plus the heavy gunfire, meant that no sleep was possible for the shift workers from the local paper mills. Boating, fishing, and even bathing from local beaches was greatly restricted. Holiday makers complained bitterly and left town in a huff.

The Council angrily wrote to the Prime Minister and also to the War Office to say the establishment of the gunnery range, so near the town was prejudicial to its best interests.

In 1930 and 1933 large chunks of shrapnel were falling on the town. One piece of shell weighing over two pounds fell beside some men working on the pier and other pieces fell on the nearby Recreation Ground and Esplanade.

A deputation was sent to the Army camp to complain. All to no avail. Even at night gun-firing would on occasions take place and the sky would be lit up by searchlights trying to locate high flying planes. An Admiralty tug named the *Haldane* was stationed at Watchet at the time to act as a patrol and safety vessel in connection with the range.

By July 1935 radio controlled planes had become technically possible and some known as Queen Bees were brought to Watchet to act as targets for the anti-aircraft gunners. The first ones were catapulted into the air from the

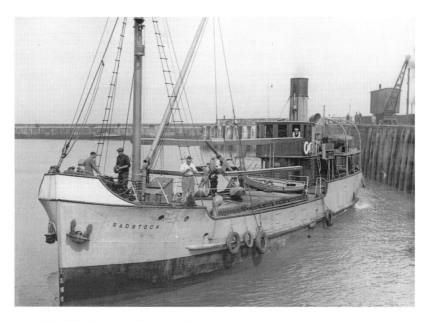

The SS "Radstock" a local ship returns to harbour with a radio controlled aeroplane known as a "Queen Bee" which had been used as a target for anti-aircraft gunners.   *(By courtesy R. Wheale)*

newly-built cruiser *H.M.S. Neptune,* which anchored a couple of miles off the harbour. Later a shore-based catapult was set up to operate from the Gunnery range at Doniford. These were indeed early and exciting days for radio controlled planes as their operation was rather hit and miss. Many people watched with trepidation as the pilotless Queen Bees zoomed eratically over the town. Some of them did indeed crash. Fortunately very little damage was done. The planes were fitted with floats, and if not shot down by the gunners would be made to alight on the water. The local steam ship *Radstock* was commissioned to recover the planes and return them to the harbour. For many years thousands of servicemen of various regiments trained at Watchet. By the 1960's however, the site had been abandoned by the military authorities. The constant erosion of the sea took its toll of the guns site, and very little trace remains. Huge circular concrete blocks which were the foundations for the guns, can today be seen lying on the beach where they fell from the eroded cliffs.

In retrospect, it can be said that the Armed Forces brought some benefits to Watchet, i.e. employment for a number of civilians. Extra money also circulated in local shops and pubs, and a large number of houses (married quarters) were eventually handed over to the local authorities. Quite a number of soldiers and airmen stationed at Watchet married local girls, bringing new blood to the area. Probably not a bad thing for a previously very tight-knit community.

Mud and Fire 1930s

The Harbours of the upper reaches of the Bristol Channel are all muddy and Watchet's harbour is no exception. The constant silting is a problem that has to be tackled periodically. A small river diverted around the harbour between tides helps to keep the main berths clear. For many years gangs of men with long handled scrapers were employed to scrape the mud into the river which then carried it out to sea. On occasions, especially if the mud had accumulated unduly, a ship would get stuck and fail to rise with the incoming tide. The ship was then said by the sailors to be sucking. The writer has seen sailors making desperate efforts to free their ships from the suction. In the case of sailing ships booms were swung heavily from one side to the other in an endeavour to shake the ship free. Steam ships if stuck would go full ahead or astern with their propellers. The trapped ship often after agonising delay would then suddenly be released and its upward leap would send a miniature but spectacular tidal wave rushing across the harbour.

The writer never saw a ship actually sink due to sucking in the mud, but according to older folk, it has been known to happen. Some Severn or Bridgwater TROWS were said in the past to have filled and sunk. This type of vessel, having no bulwarks and no hatches over its open hold would always be more liable to fill and sink than a vessel with hatches and a tarpaulin well battened down. A wise master of a TROW or a flat bottomed ship which was more liable to SUCKING than others often took the precaution of fixing a light weight chain slackly around the girth of the vessel before she went aground. Should the vessel get stuck a tug on the chain would enable water to get under the hull and she would bob up like a cork.

Prior to 1931 the only fire fighting appliance at Watchet was a hydrant stand pipe and a few lengths of hose pipe, which were taken to the fire on a hand cart.

A fire on a large steam ship loaded with Esparto grass proved impossible to extinguish with such simple equipment. But, where there's a will there's a way. Being a tidal harbour, it was possible to cut a hole low in the ship's side so that the incoming tide flooded the hold and thus extinguished the fire. As the tide receded, the water in the hold ran out again and the hole was then sealed.

After a cargo of wood pulp on the quayside had been almost completely destroyed by fire, there was a general desire to provide the town with a motor fire engine. Being saddled with huge harbour debts, the Town Council felt they could not possibly afford a new engine. However, in Feb 1931 Mr. Burnell Stephens, a local businessman and an astute salesman, offered to supply them with a second-hand fire engine for £140 and they agreed to buy after seeing a demonstration of its pumping abilities. Mr. Stephens suggested that besides fighting fires, the engine would also clear all the mud from the harbour, and some time later this idea was put to the test.

The engine was driven to the bottom of the harbour slipway when the tide was out, and taking its water from the diverted river, powerful jets were played onto the mud banks. The activities were watched by councillors and many of the townsfolk. After several hours the results were quite impressive. A large area of mud was cleared by the firemen and they were congratulated by the councillors.

A problem arose however when the engine's smooth and solid tyres were unable to get a grip on the wet and muddy slipway. Anxiety arose as the tide was now flowing, much pushing, heaving and hauling was indulged in. Eventually heavy blocks and tackle were supplied and rigged by the lifeboat crew and the engine was saved, never again did it venture into the harbour!

Harbour Dues in 1933 amounted to £1850 - 15 - 7

Harbour Dues in 1934 amounted to £1947 - 19 - 1

Imports for these two years as follows:—

	1933	1934
	tons	tons
Coal	33409	38634
Wood Pulp	25590	24049
Esparto Grass	6238	8650
Sand	331	156
Ammunition		161

63

The Smallprint

In the early 1930's trade was picking up. Large imports of Coal, Wood Pulp, and Esparto Grass as well as occasional cargoes of sand and ammunition for the nearby gunnery range, all meant "Grist to the mill". Most of the heavy loans for the rebuilding of the harbour had been paid off and the towns' ratepayers were happily anticipating some relief from their heavy burden. They were soon to be disillusioned, and without warning another mini-crisis arose. Sailors could be seen pacing up and down and heard angrily muttering "We've been hoodwinked." Businessmen and ratepayers stood talking in little groups, "We've been led up the garden path" they said. Even callow youths were echoing their elders and chirping "'Tidn Fair." The reason for their consternation was the sudden realisation that written into the *Order of 1902* which transferred the harbour from the Commissioners to the Town Council, the old Harbour Bondholders (and not the present town's ratepayers) were legally entitled to any surplus harbour revenue which accrued at the end of thirty years, viz. Sept 29th 1932. The townsfolks' hopes for a reduction in rates therefore, would not materialise.

The full significance of this had not been realised at the time of the harbour takeover, and a great deal of hostile criticism was now in full spate. "We've been done", was the cry from all around.

Another Act of Parliament was required to put things right.

The Watchet Urban District Council Act 1934 gave the council power to redeem the Bonds at 15% of their nominal value. The sum involved was nearly £26,000.

£4,200 was therefore borrowed by the council to purchase all the bonds that could be traced and to pay for the cost of the Act. From that time onwards the harbour belonged entirely to the townsfolk.

Pilotage

In reply to a query from the Elder Brethren of Trinity House in November 1933 as to the rate for pilotage at Watchet, the council replied that five shillings was allowed for the pilot from the Hobble money, (money paid to hobblers). Shortly after this, claims were made by Bridgwater pilots that, according to an ancient charter, they were legally entitled to appoint pilots for Watchet and that henceforth they intended to exercise this right with their own licenced pilots.

Watchet's hobblers, who for generations had provided pilots, were immediately up in arms.

64

"We'll chuck 'em in the harbour if they come here" was a threat uttered by angry old salts on the pier, and without a doubt they would have carried out their threat had any Bridgwater pilots appeared.

At this time, Alfred Langdon was the Watchet pilot. He is well remembered by many people as he had a very high pitched and penetrating voice and a choice selection of Watchet Blue words which he would yell at his fellow hobblers if they missed a heaving line or misunderstood his commands. It was said that Alf's loud hollering was the result of many years in command of a smack in which the only other member of the crew was almost stone deaf. On a quiet tide, sometimes in the early hours of the morning, half the town would be awakened by Alf's fruity language. Delicate ears were offended and much tut-tutting ensued. He was, however, a man who knew his job, and was a well loved character of the town.

The Council wrote to Trinity House suggesting Watchet be made a separate Pilotage district to Bridgwater and this was in due course agreed. At a meeting of the Watchet Sub Commissioners of Pilotage on 2nd December 1937, Ernest Jones Escott of Watchet was appointed as a *Trinity House Pilot* for Watchet. He was followed by Richard Allen in 1944; Hubert John Kelly, 1951; Richard Thomas Ley, 1951; William Webber, 1956; Thomas John Rawle, 1957; Ernest Gwyn Edwards, 1966; and Nigel Stokes, 1978.

Under the Pilotage Act 1987 all OUT PORT DISTRICTS administered by Trinity House will in 1988 be passed over to competent local Harbour Authorities (including Watchet).

Alfred Langdon, Watchet Pilot.

CHAPTER 6

1935 - 2000
HARBOUR TRADE REVIVAL AND TERMINATION

By 1935 the wooden section on the outer part of the East Pier due to dry rot needed extensive repairs. It was in fact almost entirely rebuilt in concrete by J. B. Edwards & Co. and cost £3,000. A warning that the West Pier also needed repair was unfortunately shelved with disastrous results.

In March 1937 disaster struck again. Gale force winds sent huge waves crashing into the West Pier. An enormous crack, in places eighteen inches wide and twenty foot deep ran for almost its entire length. Fortunately no ships were lost. Once again, to the great dismay of the ratepayers, loans were sought for approx. £17,000. The work was put in hand by George Pollard & Co. of Bridgwater on a cost plus profit basis and a considerable saving on the estimated £17,000 was made.

The main trade through the harbour at this time was still the import of wood pulp from Sweden for the paper mill at Watchet, and Esparto grass from North Africa which was also used for making paper at mills in Devonshire, a considerable amount of coal and culm was also brought in.

In the early 1930's a familiar ship leaves harbour. The "Gertrud" was a regular trader from Sweden bringing wood pulp for Watchet paper mills. The wooden structure shown was built in 1902/3 and was rebuilt in concrete in 1935.

Harbour Master Gowen Hunt (on left) calmly inspects a huge crack which appeared in the West Pier during a severe gale in 1937. A small terrier which fell into the crevice was lassoed and hauled up by its hind leg.

The *Gertrud,* a Swedish steamer of approx. 2000 tons was a most regular trader and Captain Lindh (master) made over 100 trips to Watchet in the vessel.

1938 – 1950s

In 1938 a tender to paint the lighthouse with three coats of paint for £4. 19. 0. submitted by the brothers Ben & Geoff Norman was accepted by the Council.

The second World War again brought increased coastal trade to the harbour.

Thousands of tons of coal were imported to relieve pressure on the over-loaded railways. Government policy to widely disperse the nation's food supplies resulted in cargoes of tea and other food being shipped to Watchet and stored locally in a variety of odd buildings.

Cargoes of wheat were shipped away. A large dump of scrap iron which had been collected from all over the West Country was situated on the nearby Recreation Ground and in the Mineral Yard and this was periodically shipped across the Bristol Channel to feed the Welsh smelting works.

All imports of wood pulp and Esparto grass were suspended during hostilities. The local paper mills however carried on producing paper from straw, which was collected from local farms by Burnell Stephens, a Watchet businessman.

All pleasure boating activities were suspended and coils of barbed wire were erected around the West Pier, the Esplanade and cliff tops and anywhere it was thought possible for an enemy invader to land. Coast watchers were recruited from elderly sailors and a Watch Tower was erected for them on the top of the hobblers' headquarters on the West Pier. Here they witnessed enemy aircraft bombing the docks at Barry, Cardiff and Swansea. They also saw a large section of the Mulberry Harbour which was destined for the liberation of France. It had broken adrift from its tugs in a gale of wind and it eventually sank three miles off the harbour. Also sadly witnessed was the tragic end of three sailors in a boat from Minehead who were blown up by a mine in Blue Anchor Bay. Guns were sited to defend the harbour and explosive charges were ready to be placed in position should it be thought necessary to blow it up to prevent its use by the enemy.

Mr. Gowen Hunt, the harbourmaster died in Dec. 1940 and in January 1941 Capt. Henry Redd was appointed harbourmaster. The Council resolved that the harbourmaster's salary of £70 per annum should be doubled on the understanding that he Capt. Redd would also take on the harbour signalling duties previously done by Mr. Alfred Langdon.

In 1945 the Council purchased the, by now, disused lifeboat house for £500 with the intention of providing an office for its new harbourmaster.

In 1946 trade again fell off, but Mr. W. R. Butt, a contractor for the Air

68

Ministry, sought facilities for the storage and repair of large wooden bombing targets most of which would be used at the nearby Bombing and Rocket range situated in the sea at Lilstock. In due course Mr. Butt took over the West Pier and part of the Mineral Yard and also the newly acquired lifeboat house.

For nearly twenty years the harbour provided mooring facilities for these targets which either needed repair or after repair were available and ready to be towed out to the Bombing and Rocket ranges again.

The little Clyde Puffer the "Rushlight" traded from Watchet harbour for over forty years. In the background can be seen the three cornered bombing targets which were moored in the harbour awaiting repair, or removal to Bombing Ranges. c. 1950.   *(By courtesy W. Peppin)*

Incidentally one of the vessels used by the Air Ministry to tow and moor the targets was named the *Watchmoor*. She was originally a steam herring drifter from Great Yarmouth. This ship has now been given back her original name of *Lydia Eva* and restored as a drifter by the Maritime Trust.

The bombing targets at Watchet were quite large and mostly of a distinctive three cornered shape. They were periodically placed on the harbour slipway and given a coat or two of bright red or yellow fluorescent paint which would enable them to be easily spotted by fast flying bombing and rocket firing planes when moored in the target area. On one occasion a local boatman (who shall be nameless) whose boat happened to be on the slipway at

69

Fortunately they were rotten shots

the same time as one of the targets was given a part tin of fluorescent paint which was surplus to requirements. Without thinking he painted the canopy of his boat with it. All would have been well but some time later his boat was chartered by the District Council to carry out some float tests in the Channel in connection with a proposed new sewage outfall near Lilstock. Having ascertained by telephone that no bombing or rocket firing was to take place that day the boatman, accompanied by a young Council Engineer drifted quite happily among the bombing targets. They were following and charting the floats which had drifted there. They were both happily munching their sandwiches and were not in the least perturbed when they heard a plane approaching at great speed. They both received the shock of their lives when a terrific explosion accompanied by a great upheaval of water took place quite close by. They both realised immediately that they had been misinformed as to no rocket firing taking place that day.

The boatman also regretted having painted the canopy of his boat the same fluorescent colour as the targets. The throttle was opened wide and the boat streaked at full speed out of the range which was by now receiving rockets thick and fast from numerous other follow-on planes. When they returned to shore the Council's Engineer remonstrated angrily over the phone with the target range authorities, but got no satisfactory explanation as to who was to blame. The boatman meanwhile kept a low profile and decided to repaint the boat the very next day.

70

In Sept 1949 yet another collapse of part of the East Wharf occurred and Mr. Humby, a consulting engineer recommended the use of steel piling to repair the breach in the harbour wall. Another loan of £6,000 was required for this work. Meanwhile the old problem of silting was again causing concern, large steamships were at times unable to get into berth and occasionally got stuck on the huge mud banks which had gradually built up in the harbour and necessitated waiting for the tides to rise before they could move. Obviously something had to be done to remedy this state of affairs.

In 1950 Mr. Harold Kimber from Highbridge was engaged to clear the harbour mud with a device that had previously successfully cleared the mud from the Marine Lake at Weston Super Mare. Mr. Kimber quoted the sum of £2,750 for the work plus £250 for clearing any large obstructions. The Wansbrough Paper Co., the major user of the port at this time, agreed to pay one third of the cost. A boiler and steam winch were set up on the West Pier with long wire ropes which were slung across the harbour, and a scraping device was heaved to and fro. Some mud was shifted and cleared, but the heavy, long settled silt at the bottom was almost rock hard, and could not be moved with the gear. Mr. Kimber's contract was therefore terminated.

In 1952 the Wansbrough Paper Co., arranged for Messrs. Blackford of Calne to undertake the task of mud clearance. In return the Council agreed not to increase harbour dues for three years.

A large mechanical digger and three dumper trucks working between tides excavated thousands of tons of silt which in places was over seven feet deep and dumped it outside the harbour.

In March 1953 Capt. Harry Redd, the harbourmaster, died and from April 1st Capt. Thomas Ley was appointed harbourmaster at a salary of £200 per annum plus 5% of commission on dues above £1200. Capt. Ley was at this time the appointed Trinity House Pilot at Watchet, and he carried on this work together with his duties of Harbourmaster.

In 1953 the SS *Rushlight* which had traded from the harbour for over forty years sailed on her last voyage to the breaker's yard at Llanelly. Her place was taken by the SS *Arran Monarch* a ship of similar size and appearance and she carried on the *Rushlight's* job of bringing small coal or culm for the paper mills mainly from Cardiff. She was not to stay long for the coal fired boilers of the paper mill were soon to be gradually phased out and superceded by new oil burning boilers.

The mud problem was tackled again in 1955. The Wansbrough Paper Co. who were almost the only user of the harbour at this time obtained a small mud clearing barge from the Bridgwater river. It was named the *Perseverance*. Fitted with high pressure water pumps it discharged a powerful jet of water at the mud banks. The resulting slurrified or watered down mud was carried out to sea by the river which was diverted around the harbour for this purpose. The harbourmaster, Thomas Ley and his brother Preston were actively engaged on this task and for many years the harbour berths were kept clear.

The SS "Ring", a Swedish steamer, centre, with the Watchet owned
SS "Arran Monarch" on the right and mud barge "Perseverance" on the
left. c. 1950's.

The Legal Quay

Efforts by the Harbour Authority to increase trade and to import more and
varied cargoes received a temporary setback in 1958. The landing of cargoes
of potatoes on the East Pier and Wharf according to some zealous Customs
and Excise officials could not be allowed at Watchet without a special permit
which they were reluctant to provide. Ship broker Alfred Allen and Harbourmaster Thomas Ley who were doing all they could to encourage new trade were
both hopping mad at what appeared to them to be a lot of red tape. They
called on and complained to Percival Risdon the Town Clerk who delved into
the harbour records and gleefully produced an ancient document which
proved Watchet's Harbour had a *Legal Quay* and could therefore quite law-
fully import not only potatoes but hundreds of other listed commodities:

Included in the list were :—

Cargoes of Cannon Balls or Guano
Hogsheads of Wine, Brandy or Rum
Chests of Oranges and Lemons
Kilderkins of Ale or Porter
Dickers of Leather and Arsenic
Cwts of Manna or Manna Croup
Bushels of Apples or Pears
Barrels of Pitch or Tar
Bundles of Treenails or Humells
Boxes of Divi Divis

72

Bales of Tobacco
Firkins of Mustard
and Bladders of Snuff — (to boot.)

When contronted with this formidable list it was said that the Customs &
Excise officials were for a while quite speechless; but *after* careful scrutiny
they pointed out that the Legal Quay referred to on the old document, was
situated at the old West Pier and therefore the East Pier and Wharf having
been built much later, would not be considered Legal Quays.

Urgent consideration was then given to the possibility of again making
use of the old *Legal Quay* at the West Pier for landing the potatoes. Considerable dredging would be necessary to enable it to be used, furthermore the
West Pier was not very suitable for large lorries to negotiate.

Fortunately common sense prevailed and a compromise was reached.
For the Customs & Excise officials eventually suggested that potatoes and
many, but not all, of the other named goods could be unloaded or loaded
on the East Pier & Wharf *provided* the Harbour Authority relinquished their
Legal Quay rights on the West Pier. This was agreed and a few years later
a comfortable new office overlooking the harbour was erected by the Council
for the use of the Customs & Excise officials to enable them to carry out
their duties.

Minehead Harbour *Legal Quay* rights were also surrendered to the Customs
Authorities shortly after those of Watchet.

For hundreds of years Watchet had been a ship-owning community.

In 1961 many folk were saddened when the last locally owned little ship,
the *Arran Monarch,* was sold away, to new owners at Bude. She had been
owned by the local paper mills and had almost daily brought coal to feed the
boilers at the mill. Now after new oil fired boilers had been installed, she was
surplus to requirements.

Jack Allen (master) and his crew had to seek employment ashore.

During the winter of 1962/63 severe weather conditions again brought
harbour trade to a standstill. This was caused not by gale force winds as had
happened many times before but by the lowest temperatures ever known at
Watchet within living memory.

The foreshore was covered by a mass of ice floes and the strong and
continuous Easterly wind drove these floes into the harbour entrance which
faces to the East.

The ice floes then built up more and more with each successive tide, until
they were several feet thick and quite spectacular.

A large ship the *Admiral Bastian,* was for a few days held firmly against
the Quay wall and unable to sail.

She was also unable to take on fresh water supplies as water mains buried
deep in the pier had frozen solid. So cold was the weather that all the seaweed on the rocky foreshore died leaving the rocks completely bare. Limpets

Ice floes in the harbour in the severe winter of 1962/63.

(By courtesy P. Norton)

on the rocks were all killed and for several years no prawns could be found in the rock pools along the shore.

By 1962 all imports of coal had ceased and shipments of woodpulp were coming to an end. Scandinavian woodpulp for the paper mills had been superceded by Canadian pulp and this was shipped across the Atlantic in large ships which were unloaded at major ports, usually Avonmouth. It was then forwarded to Watchet by road transport. The Esparto grass trade was also slipping away to other small competing ports in South Devon. These ports were situated nearer to the paper mills which required it. The outlook for the harbour at this time was bleak indeed.

However two National events were evolving which were greatly to affect the future of the harbour as follows:

Event No. 1

The unloading and loading of ships in most British ports had for generations been carried out by unregistered dockers employed on a casual basis, as and when required and who therefore had no security of employment. Understandably much resentment was felt at this insecurity and after much Union pressure, a National Dock Labour Scheme was set up which registered the dockers and henceforth Port employers were required by law to guarantee them full employment. Some of the smaller ports including Watchet for various reasons were not included in the Scheme.

Despite much improved conditions and substantial pay packets, dockers

74

at many of the larger ports continued to be dissatisfied and would strike at the least excuse, consequently ships were often held up for long periods.

Small wonder therefore that some shipping firms cast their eyes enviously in the direction of the few remaining small and unregistered ports where labour relations were more reasonable.

Event No. 2

By 1962 British Rail was under the direction of Dr. Beeching who was ruthlessly cutting uneconomic railway services throughout the country. Consequently at the time goods services on the branch line serving Watchet were brought to an abrupt end.

Prophets of Doom woefully proclaimed that this would be the final nail in the Watchet harbour coffin.

How wrong they were ! !

The termination of Railway goods traffic resulted in the release of the vital land adjoining the harbour so necessary for the storage of cargoes. This land which the Harbour Authority had sold to the Railway Co. in 1861 for £50 was now once again available to them.

Its price together with a small goods shed and a long strip of land adjacent to Harbour Road was £10,000.

It was realised that this land was the key to harbour trade and the Council did not hesitate to acquire it.

Space was now available for warehouses and cargo space and before long shipping firms and Companies were showing great interest in Watchet's little harbour.

In 1963 the West Pier and part of the harbour adjoining was leased to the newly formed West Somerset Shipping Co. who proposed to carry out ship-breaking there.

No ships were actually broken up by this Company which in retrospect was perhaps most fortunate for it would have been a very noisy, dirty and ugly operation.

Samual Tutton & Sons, Stevedores of Avonmouth and Charles M. Willie (Shipping) Ltd. of Cardiff set up offices at Watchet in 1967 and prepared to do business.

Port modernisation grants were sought to level and develop the newly purchased Railway land and both these Companies were each leased areas of the land.

Suddenly, ships, ships and yet more ships came sailing into the harbour.

Gangs of men were taken on to unload cargoes of fish meal, bone meal, fertilizers, timber and goods of every description.

A mountain of scrap iron for export grew to a great height on the East Wharf.

Dozens of huge articulated lorries appeared, causing traffic jams and confusion, some shed their loads of timber in the streets, for Watchet's dockers at this time were inexperienced in timber loading techniques.

Fork lift trucks rushed screaming around the harbour and new high speed diesel powered cranes were set up; these were a far cry from the old steam cranes which for years had wheezed and puffed in leisurely fashion as they loaded cargoes of wood pulp or coal and esparto grass into horse drawn trucks.

The volume and tonnage of goods being shipped through the harbour was now higher than for many years. New harbourside offices were built for Customs Officials and also for the harbour master. New showers and toilets for the dockers were provided. In Harbour Road, a trailer park was laid out in the hope of easing traffic congestion and a large warehouse, weighbridge and offices were erected by C. M. Willie Ltd. one of the shipping companies.

A prominent lady councillor considered the busy harbour scene could be still further improved if the Harbour Master, Thomas Ley, could be persuaded to wear an official Harbour Masters hat.

Her wishes were rejected by that officer who normally never wore a hat. He declared the hat would be a nuisance particularly as he liked to scratch his head when making important decisions and also that it would blow off in the wind and be a complete waste of money. The harbour master stuck to his guns and remained hatless.

Over many years thousands of pounds of ratepayers money had been spent repairing and strengthening the harbour but now due to inflation hundreds of thousands of pounds were required. The piers and wharfs were

Harbour master Thomas Ley.

76

to be strengthened as never before and those ratepayers who believed the harbour goose would now lay them some golden eggs were again to be sadly disillusioned.

Intense rivalry between the shipping companies soon became apparent. Some ships chartered by one company had the words WATCHET LINE printed on their sides in huge letters.

Not to be outdone the other company named one of its chartered ships the WATCHET STAR, other ships chartered and named by them at this time were the Aveiro Star, Douro Star and Lisbon Star. These names complimented the main ports to which they traded.

Sad to relate the latter named ship caught fire late one night while berthed in the harbour and her master was burned to death in his cabin.

A considerable trade to Portugal developed mainly with the export of crated motor car parts, tractors and farm machinery, zinc, lead, copper and steel, as well as china clay and whisky.

Return cargoes were of box wood, cork, hardboard, chipboard, linen, wine, paper, or wood pulp, also came cargoes of bones from Pakistan — soft wood from the Azores, feeding stuffs, fertilizers and general cargo from Continental ports. In 1972 a complete prefabricated hotel was shipped direct to Gibraltar.

It was about this time possibly as an aid to lorry drivers that WATCHET DOCKS appeared on road signs leading to the harbour. It seems to the writer regrettable to replace the traditional and correct title HARBOUR with the harsh sounding and unwelcoming word DOCKS.

Big business had arrived at last. Harbour trade was literally booming, but Watchet's residents had been rudely awakened from their slumbers and by no means was everyone happy at the increased trade and all it entailed.

A heavy price had to be paid. Free harbourside car parking could no longer be allowed and restriction of pedestrian access to both piers was greatly resented, particularly onto the West Pier much loved by anglers, prawners and local people who for generations had promenaded up and down its length. They had come to look on it as their own amenity area and were most reluctant to give it up.

Considerable dredging alongside the West Pier was carried out by the Bristol and West Shipping Co. who by now had taken over the interests of both Messrs. Tutton and the West Somerset Shipping Co.

This dredging enabled ships to be berthed alongside this pier and discharged and loaded. Chaotic traffic snarl-ups resulted, for narrow Swain Street and Market Street were barely able to cope with the ever-increasing holiday traffic, much less the huge juggernauts which now came charging their way through, en route to the West pier.

Inevitably property was damaged, nerves were frayed and the patience of residents and shopkeepers was sorely tried.

Councillors and Port Officials who ventured into the street were verbally abused and angry letters were written to the local Press.

All to no avail, Events now had to take their course.

For many years, gradually and quietly and almost unnoticed, a substantial tourist business had been building up in and around the town.

It was realised that this would be in jeopardy if suggested road widening schemes were put in hand, for this would have destroyed the quaint and narrow little streets — the very things that the tourists came to see and appreciate.

Thankfully no road widening took place, Swain Street and Market Street and most of the old part of the town survived.

In 1974 the Boundary Commission was set up by the Government to end anomalies in the size and structure of local authorities.

Generally speaking small authorities such as Watchet were directed to join with others to make bigger and supposedly more efficient centres of local government. As previously explained Watchet's Urban Authority had been formed in 1902 in order to finance the rebuilding of the harbour without which its main industries could not continue.

By 1974 local industries no longer depended on the harbour or made use of it, yet more tonnage and of greater variety than anyone could remember was now being shipped through the port.

The harbour was at this time taken over by the new and larger authority, namely — The West Somerset District Council. Many of the Officials and workforce connected with the harbour were already drawn from this larger district.

Ownership of the harbour with its debts and ever hopefully its future benefits were therefore spread over and shared with this larger community.

During 1974 Harbourmaster Thomas Ley retired due to ill health and his place was taken by Capt. Christofell Muller of Bridgwater.

By 1975 the Bristol and West Shipping Co. had ceased trading completely.

They had defaulted in payments on the lease of the West pier and also the cargo storage spaces held by them on the East Wharf and off Harbour Road. These properties as well as their offices on the Esplanade were therefore repossessed by the newly formed District Council.

The West Pier was not relet for shipping purposes. It was decided to retain it as a public amenity area and hopefully it will remain so.

In Oct. 1975 the County Council after calling a public meeting to sound local opinion decided that the old part of Watchet including its narrow streets and the harbour should be designated a Conservation Area.

Meanwhile shipping operations continued steadily on the more easily accessible East Pier and East Wharf by the one remaining Shipping Co.: C. M. Willie through their subsidiary Watchet Marine Ltd.

The local road haulage firm of S & M Street had also by now amalgamated with this company.

A large lorry park was developed just outside the town and this greatly eased the traffic problems which had caused so much resentment.

Neither of the cargo storage spaces on the East Wharf or in Harbour Road vacated by the defaulting company were reserved for any possible new Port operators but were leased almost immediately to the one remaining firm of C. M. Willie Ltd. Time and future historians will doubtless decide whether the Port Authority were wise at the time to place all their eggs in one basket?

Be that as it may most people were thankful that one of the Shipping firms was continuing to trade, and were even more pleased to see them purchase and operate their own fleet of ships again from Watchet.

The sight of ships flying the Red Ensign had for many years become all too rare. Now it was once again possible for Watchet lads to sign on and sail from their home port on a British ship.

The Celtic "Endeavour" approaching the harbour with a cargo of timber and cork from Portugal, 1984.

The first ship in the new Willie fleet arrived in May 1978. She was named the *Celtic Venture* and was of 1,954 tons gross. She traded mainly to Portugal. Her last voyage to Watchet was in Feb. 1982 after which she was sold away.

The *Celtic Endeavour* of 1,428 tons gross arrived in Feb. 1979.

In 1980 the *Celtic Crusader* of 698 tons gross joined the fleet. This ship was formerly named the *Supremity* and had belonged to Everards. She was equipped with very heavy lifting derricks amidships and was particularly suitable for handling containers. Container traffic was at the time a substantial part of harbour trade.

79

Being thus equipped this vessel was considered by the powers that be to be very suitable for use in taking supplies to the Falklands garrison. She left Watchet in Aug. 1983 and after loading supplies, sailed for the Falklands under the command of Capt. Sully. The 2nd Officer was Ian Rewe, a young man of Watchet.

The *Celtic Crusader* was sold and renamed the KORIMU.

Two more ships joined the Willie Fleet

The *Celtic Voyager* of 924 tons gross arrived in May 1984 and her sister ship, *Celtic Mariner* of the same tonnage came to Watchet in August 1984.

Harbour activities in the 1980's were not entirely confined to the commercial shipping, for a considerable number of boats and yachts made good use of those areas of the harbour which were clear of shipping. An active local boat owners' Association laid out heavy chain moorings and membership of the club was open to any ratepayer or resident in the new enlarged community. Harbour dues were payable to the Habour Authority depending on the size of the craft.

On occasions as in days of yore, water sports and raft races were organised by the Association usually in aid of R.N.L.I. funds.

During the late 1970's and 1980's national recession hit and destroyed large numbers of industries throughout the country. Watchet did not go unscathed.

Two small factories ceased trading and many were unemployed.

Fortunately the town's main industry the paper mills survived.

The tonnage of cargoes shipped through the harbour had peaked in 1980 at 141,024 tons, but had fallen considerably by 1983 when a number of dockers and lorry drivers were laid off.

In April 1986, C. M. Willie bought the *Celtic Challenger* ex *Argo Valour* 3200 tonnes deadweight. The *Celtic Endeavour* was sold in 1986 and renamed *Dawpool.*

The number of vessels managed by the Company increased from two to six vessels in the handy 1200/1800 tonnes deadweight size.

The main imports in 1987 were timber from Portugal, the main exports waste paper to Turkey and Spanish Morocco.

Interesting reminders of Watchet's historic past took place in 1988 when some unusual harbour activities took place. These were staged to commemorate the millennium of Viking raids which had taken place at Watchet a thousand years previously. Fearsome Vikings with horns on their helmets landed from their longboats. They engaged in terrific battles with defending Saxons, much to the enjoyment of thousands of spectators crowded around the harbourside. Other activities that year, included the use of a ducking stool by Watchet's long established Court Leet. (All part of community celebrations known as WATCHET 1000.)

From its peak in 1980 trade through the harbour had continued to decline.

This was much regretted by the townfolk and many visitors who delighted in seeing the loading and unloading of the large ocean going and colourful ships.

In January, 1993 most local people were devastated to hear that Watchet Marine Co. Ltd., the subsidiary of C. M. Willie Co. Ltd., had gone into liquidation, and that the dockers' jobs terminated with only two hours notice. Watchet Marine at that time was the major user of the port and the last of the Willie ships to leave the harbour on 11th January was the M.V. CELTIC VENTURE II. Most of Watchet's regular trade was then immediately transferred by C.M. Willie Co. Ltd. to Avonmouth Docks.

There was, however, still some hope of trade revival. Channel Sand Co. Ltd., (Managing Director George Roberts) had in recent months started to import cargoes of sand dredged from the Culver sandbanks – only a few miles offshore. Other cargoes brought in by the Company for local agricultural use were of calsified seaweed from Falmouth, and fertilisers from Belfast. On 12th March the Company imported quite a large shipment of sand. This was brought in by the 'WELSH PIPER' – a self discharging dredger. This versatile vessel, after quickly discharging her cargo onto the East Wharf, was able to leave port on the same tide. Her entire cargo of over 1,000 tons was destined for use on building a new hospital at Musgrove Park, Taunton.

In April Channel Sand Co. Ltd., applied to the Port Authorities for a short term lease of part of the wharf on which to store cargoes. The Authority – for legal reasons felt unable to grant this and regrettably no further cargoes were ever imported by the Company.

In 1995/6 an enterprising venture to fish for whelks in the Bristol Channel took place. At that time, strange tho' it may seem, there was an insatiable demand for these particular shellfish in Middle and Far Eastern countries. Tons of whelks were exported from this country. Mr Philip Bowditch, a fish merchant of Taunton fitted out the fair sized beam trawler 'MICHELLE LOUISA' which he based at Watchet. After a number of trial runs, whelk grounds were located off the Welsh coast. Mr Bowditch had in mind to set up a processing plant on the harbourside where freshly caught shellfish could be cooked and processed for export.

Unfortunately just at that time the 'SEA EMPRESS' – a huge oil tanker ran onto rocks while entering Milford Haven. Thousands of tons of crude oil spilled out contaminating miles of shoreline. By order of the Ministry of Fisheries all fishing for shellfish in the Bristol Channel had to cease.

In August 1996 the 'MICHELLE LOUISA' left Watchet and fished out of Cherbourg with a French crew. After a few months she left France for Brixham and at present is successfully beam trawling out of that port.

During 1996 two unusual vessels moored alongside the West Pier for a few days. The first was the sail training ship – 'ROYALIST' which was much admired and boarded by many visitors and locals. The second was the

Theatre ship 'FITZ-CARALDO' which called at ports all around Britain giving much appreciated live shows.

Occasional summer-time cruises to Bristol Channel ports or islands can still be taken from Watchet aboard the motor vessels 'BALMORAL' and 'OLDENBURG'. They operate from the West Pier.

The training ship 'Royalist' rigged as a brig entering the harbour in 1996.
(By courtesy Fred Routledge and Bosun Ted Edwards)

APPENDIX

Even before the shipping trade ended, rumours were circulating around the town that a change of use of the harbour – to form a water-retaining marina – was being contemplated by the Port Authorities.

Some people considered the shipping trade would probably not return and that in their opinion a fair-sized marina with floating boats would attract many more visitors to the town. 'Especially so' they considered 'as the unsightly mud in the tidal habour would no longer be visible, and Watchet should turn to tourism for its future prosperity and many more jobs'.

This view was strongly opposed by others who wished the harbour to remain available for any future shipping. Many folk considered a marina at Watchet would provide very few jobs and was unlikely to be popular because of it limited tidal access. Old Hobblers and 'Doomsters' hanging around the harbour predicted gloomily that it would constantly silt-up and might well become a White Elephant.

Sincere and candid opinions for or against a change of use caused heated arguments, even among friends. The whole town became divided as never before in its history. Many letters strongly favouring or opposing the idea appeared in local newspapers.

In August 1993, taken aback by the diversity of opinion, West Somerset District Council who were at this time the owners of the harbour, decided to commission the well-known consultants – Coopers and Lybrand – to carry out a feasibility study of the town and harbour.

In due course the experts gave their opinion that the shipping trade was unlikely to recover. They gave several reasons for this including insurance problems and poor road connections to and from the port. They also found that handling charges at neighboring ports were twenty-five per cent lower than Watchet. Advertisements recently placed in a maritime journal to promote the harbour and its facilities had brought a number of enquiries from interested shipping firms but none were prepared to trade under the existing pre-conditions.

After studying the consultants' report the councillors made the momentous – although not unanimous – decision to convert the harbour into a marina. Much could be written of the further spirited arguments between the marina enthusiasts and those who opposed the harbour closure. The controversy ws to go on and on for seven years.

During November, 1999, a lengthy far reaching and costly Public Enquiry was held at Watchet and eventually on July 14th 2000 a Harbour Revision Order was issued by the Government. This in effect closed Watchet Harbour to commercial shipping for ever and enabled the construction of the marina to go ahead.

Government grants and European Funding to help finance the construction had already been negotiated by the Council Officers, but their Lottery bid for funding was unsuccessful. In all, the cost of the construction was to exceed five million pounds. The firm of Dean and Dyball Constructions was selected to design, build and to operate the 260 berth marina. Work started on October 2nd, 2000 and on July 18th 2001 Watchet's Marina – embracing local and visiting yachts was declared 'Open' by the renowned yachtsman Sir Robin Knox-Johnson.

Sir Robin Knox-Johnson opens the marina. *(by courtesy Steve Gusscott)*

Aerial view showing the newly constructed water retaining Marina on the right *(By courtesy Dr A Dayani)*

Part Two

CHAPTER 7

SAILORS' SOCIETIES AND THE COASTGUARDS

Watchet Hobblers

No book of Watchet harbour should be written without including the story of the Hobblers.

They are the men who for many generations have assisted in the berthing, mooring and unmooring of ships. This was particularly important in the days of sail. Small sailing ships when under way in the open sea can be handled by a comparatively small crew! In fact Ketches and Smacks often sailed on long voyages with only two or three men aboard. But when these ships were leaving the harbour many tasks were required to be done all at the same time, such as taking in and stowing away mooring warps, towing or warping the vessel to the pier head, or to a buoy which was permanently moored outside and to the Eastward of the harbour entrance. Hoisting sails, and releasing moorings all at the critical time, to enable the vessel to get clear of the pier-heads. The assistance of additional skilled men at such a time was necessary and welcomed.

Similarly a ship approaching harbour would accept a boat load of hobblers, who would if necessary advise on piloting and help to lower sails or anchor, and then tow or winch the ship into berth. This was often a most laborious job and all done by man-power alone in all weathers. Prior to the great up-surge in trade in the 1860's the hobblers consisted of three separate gangs of men with three separate rowing boats named the *Rodney,* the *Telegraph* and the *Frolic.* They were owned by different families and competed against each other.

A vessel approaching the harbour would take on only the first boat of hobblers to contact her, and for their assistance would pay a set charge dependent on the tonnage of the vessel and whether she was coastwise or foreign. The payment was known as the hobble. This system had existed for generations and tales have been handed down of the three hobble boats racing to be the first to board an approaching ship. Secret information of a ship's expected time of arrival was whispered around town. Hobblers crept silently around the harbour at night with sacking tied around their boots and rowed out with muffled oars, hoping thus to steal a march on their sleeping rivals. Sometimes one of the boats would be rowed many miles down channel even as far as Porlock Bay or to the West Culvers seeking expected vessels bound for Watchet. But these enterprising moves did not always

A boat load of hobblers having warped the ketch "Electric" out of the
harbour, leave her to attend another vessel. *(By courtesy Michael Bouquet)*

pay off for on some occasions the Watchet bound ship did not see the tiny
hobble boat and its frantically waving crew, and made all speed to Watchet
to be attended by one of the rival gangs, who had remained hanging about
on the pier.

Henry Chidgey, master mariner, Landlord of the London Inn.
(By courtesy S. W. Norman)

Tempers got frayed especially when the unsuccessful crew returned
wearily to the harbour and were jeered at by those who had remained at
Watchet. The rule that those who had attended the vessel on her arrival could
also take her out, did not help to smooth things over. False information of
ships' movements were leaked to confound the enemies: even little children
were trained to tell lies. Inevitably tempers snapped, angry taunts were
uttered and at times blows were struck.

In 1863, obviously on a day when tempers had cooled, Henry Chidgey,
the landlord of the London Inn and himself a master mariner and ship owner,
together with others, called all three gangs together. It was pointed out that

the harbour trade was increasing and that there would be enough work for all three gangs and therefore no need for arguments or fighting. It was proposed that the three boats be put into a club for the mutual benefit of all members. This was agreed and a club was formed and called The United Sailors' Society. Bearing in mind the early date and circumstances, the formation of this self help friendly society with considerable welfare benefits, was unique and reflects great credit and a remarkable sense of community spirit among Watchet's seafaring men.

The Society published a booklet containing its rules and benefits and a list of Watchet owned ships and the amount of Hobble that would be collected from each one. Very few of the original rule booklets have survived but one was kindly given to the writer by Mr. Jack Hurley of Williton. The rules are interesting and quaint and deserve to be republished in full *(See following pages)*.

By adhering strictly to the rules the Society prospered. The family feuds ended from that time on and Watchet was a happy community. Every Whit Monday a procession of Sailors marched to church wearing rosettes and carrying their own official wooden ceremonial staffs which were topped with a brass emblem in the form of an anchor.

A report in *The West Somerset Free Press*, June 11 1881 :

"Watchet United Sailors on Whit Monday marched in procession headed with St. Decuman's Brass Band and large flags. After church the band played the anthem 'Jerusalem my glorious home' to the admiration of all present. Procession was again formed and the streets of the town paraded. The procession then wound its way to the clubroom at the London Inn where a first-class dinner was served by Mr. & Mrs. Chidgey in their usual good style of catering. In the course of the afternoon the streets were again paraded and afterwards the members returned to the club room where dancing etc was indulged in. The band played some choice selections of music and gave general satisfaction and the proceedings passed off in a respectable manner."

In this day and age it is laughable to think of the cunning and subterfuge adopted by the hobblers in order to earn just a few pence each, but in those mean days of no dole, or welfare, the choice was to find any low paid or menial work, or starve.

In 1890 the United Sailors erected a new Watch House on the West Pier. It was used for watching and waiting for ships, also for paying out the hobble and for meetings.

By 1946 the sickness and other benefits had long since been discontinued as had the church parades and annual dinner. The name of the society had been changed to the Watchet Hobblers Association and a new set of rules drawn up. No upper age limit was set in the new rules and up until the 1950's old salts of over 80 years of age could be seen on the pier making fast or casting off mooring warps and springs.

RULES

OF THE

UNITED SAILORS'

SOCIETY,

HELD AT

THE LONDON INN, WATCHET,

IN THE COUNTY OF SOMERSET.

Established March 25th, 1863.

WATCHET:

PRINTED BY A. K. BALDWIN, BOOKSELLER AND STATIONER.

M.DCC.LXIII.

89

United Sailors' Society.

This is to Certify,

That _Thomas Wheeler_

is a Member of the above Society.

W. W. Escott Secretary.

Date, _May 13th — 1863_

RULES.

AT a Meeting of the Shareholders of the Hobble Boats, viz., the *Frolic, Telegraph,* and *Rodney,* belonging to the port of Watchet, held at the London Inn, on the 18th day of March, 1863, it was resolved and agreed that the three Boats be put into a club, to be called the "United Sailors' Society," for the mutual benefit of those who now hold a share or shares in the three Boats. Any shareholder objecting to become a member of the society shall be paid such amount as the share may now be worth, or may sell the share to any other party who is eligible to become a member. The society to be governed by the following Rules:

1. That the society be called the "United Sailors' Society," and that its meetings be held at the London Inn, Watchet, on the second Wednesday in every month, commencing from the 25th day of March, 1863.

2. That a committee of twelve members be appointed half-yearly, for the management of the business of the society, and they shall appoint a secretary, who shall be paid the sum of fourpence per member each year, and give his services at all times that the business of the society require.

3. That the secretary and such of the committee as are able shall attend at the society's room on every monthly meeting night, at the hour of seven in the evening, and remain until nine, p.m., from Lady-day to Michaelmas; and from six to eight from Michaelmas to Lady-day.

4. That the earnings of the boats be put into a box, and that the boat's share shall be the full share of a man, according to the amount of hobble; and all odd pence shall be added to the box. Each member shall also contribute to the funds of the society the sum of sixpence per month. That James Nurcombe be appointed collector of all monies to which the boats may be entitled, and shall convey the same unto Isaac Allen, who shall

keep the box, and also a book for entering all monies deposited in such box; and this box shall be brought to the society's room every monthly meeting night.

5. That a general box shall be provided, having three different locks and keys, for the safe custody of all monies, books, &c., belonging to the society. That such box be kept at the society's meeting house, and be in the custody of the landlord of the house, who shall also pay all legal demands on the society from month to month, and the committee shall determine what amount shall be advanced to him for that purpose.

6. That the total funds of the society shall accumulate for twelve months, before any sick benefit shall be paid; but should any member or member's wife die before the expiration of the twelvemonth, the sum of two pounds shall be paid.

7. That after the expiration of the first year, every member during sickness shall receive the sum of five shillings per week for twelve months, from the date of the notice of the commencement of such illness, and half that amount as long as he may continue unable to follow his usual employment.

But no member shall receive sick pay for illness caused by any indirect manner of life, or for any injury or disorder arising from a broil or from improper conduct.

8. That on the death of a free member or his wife, the sum of five pounds shall be paid, and should he have been a member of the society for five years, he shall receive the sum of seven pounds, which amount shall be the total sum paid by the society.

9. That each member shall contribute the sum of sixpence to the funds of the society on the death of a member or member's wife.

10. That should the funds of the society increase sufficiently, the sum of two shillings per week for life, shall be paid to every male member of the society on his attaining the age of sixty-five years; but such payment shall not in any case commence before the 25th of March, 1867.

11. That no person be admitted a member of this society who is under fourteen or above forty years of age; and that the entrance fee for admission

shall be ten shillings and sixpence. Each member shall also pay threepence for the book of articles.

12. That should any member be detected in cheating the boats, or in any way defrauding the society's funds, he shall be fined for the first offence the sum of five shillings, and for the second, the sum of ten shillings; and should it occur a third time, his name shall be erased from the society's books, without any money being returned. The fines shall be paid to the secretary the first monthly night after being demanded, or the member shall be excluded. All fines shall be added to the society's funds.

13. That an annual dinner shall be provided for the members of the society on Whit-Monday, for which each member shall contribute his share. Members unable to attend, may have their dinner at their own residence.

14. Should any dispute arise between the members it shall be settled by the committee of the society for the time being.

15. That if any member be found guilty of felony he shall be excluded from the society.

16. That when the funds of the society shall exceed the sum of fifty pounds, the members shall decide whether the surplus over and above that amount shall be equally divided between themselves, or be invested, at interest, on proper security.

17. That if at any time hereafter it shall be found necessary to alter or abolish any of these rules, or to make new ones, a special meeting of the members shall be called, and the consent of a majority obtained, to the proposed alteration or amendment.

Signed, on behalf of the Members,

JOHN WEDLAKE,
RICHARD ALLEN,
JOSEPH PITTAWAY.

JOHN WESCOMBE, *Secretary.*

Baldwin, Printer and Bookseller, Watchet.

AMOUNT OF HOBBLE FOR WATCHET VESSELS.

ENTERING AND LEAVING THE PORT.	If above 20 tons cargo. s. d.	Under 20 tons or in proportion. s. d.
Kelso	8 0	4 6
Richard	5 6	3 6
Friends smack	5 0	3 0
Hawk	8 0	4 6
Thomasine & Mary	6 6	4 0
Ocean	6 6	4 0
Express	6 6	4 0
Gannet	6 6	4 0
Friends, schooner	6 6	4 0
Quiver	6 6	3 6
Tartar	5 6	3 6
Mary Lauder	5 6	3 6
Ann	7 0	4 0
Thomas and Sarah	5 6	3 6
Princess	8 0	4 6
Ceres	5 6	3 6
Charles Phillips	5 0	3 0
Union Packet	5 0	3 6
Tom	4 0	2 9
Hellen	7 0	4 6
Star of the West	9 0	6 0
Providence	8 6	6 0
Friendship	8 0	5 0
Lloyds	3 6	2 6
Laurina	3 0	1 6
Abeona	3 6	1 6
Fortitude	6 6	4 0

COASTING VESSELS.

		£ s. d.
20 to 30	Tons Register	0 10 0
30 to 40	,,	0 12 0
40 to 50	,,	0 14 0
50 to 60	,,	0 16 0
60 to 70	,,	0 18 0
70 to 80	,,	1 0 0
80 to 90	,,	1 2 0
90 to 100	,,	1 4 0
100 to 110	,,	1 6 0
110 to 120	,,	1 8 0
120 to 130	,,	1 10 0
130 to 140	,,	1 12 0
140 to 150	,,	1 14 0
150 to 160	,,	1 16 0
160 to 170	,,	1 18 0
170 to 180	,,	2 0 0
180 to 190	,,	2 2 0
190 to 200	,,	2 4 0
200 to 210	,,	2 6 0

And 2s. additional for every 10 tons.

Coasting Vessels, coming in ballast, are subject to a reduction of one-fourth of the above Rates.

PRINTED BY A. K. BALDWIN, BOOKSELLER &C, WATCHET.

A strong South Westerly wind in the Western Approaches causes a heavy ground swell in the Bristol Channel, this in turn causes boats and ships in Watchet's exposed harbour to surge to and fro. Large steamers of around 2000 tons which were quite usual at this time needed to be moored with massive coir hawsers which were 24 inches in circumference and were known locally as junks. They were especially made for the harbour by Messrs. Waddon, Ropemakers of Bridgwater. These Junks when wet weighed very heavily and the hobblers needed blocks and tackle to haul them back onto the quay after the ships had cast off and sailed. An extra charge was made for the use of the Junks by the Harbour Authority. It was not made compulsory for the ships' masters to take them, but few refused for they knew a surging ship would snap its own wire ropes which had no give or stretch.

A curious method was used for the election of new hobblers.

A meeting was called at the Watch House where the name of the applicant was read out and proposed and seconded. Then each member, who had previously been given a handful of black and white beans, was asked to vote by placing either a black or a white bean in a bucket which was passed around. The white bean was favourable and the black was against the applicant. The black and white beans in the bucket were then separated, carefully counted, and the applicant was either rejected or after paying his entrance fee, made a hobbler.

By 1970 most of the old sailing ships men were dead and the number of hobblers quickly fell. New nylon lightweight ropes replaced the heavy junks and this enabled mooring and unmooring ships to be done by just two or three men. The Watch House had fallen into disrepair and was sold by tender. It now forms part of an adjoining cottage.

The Watchet Shipowners' Society

The everpresent likelihood of the loss of small sailing ships by stress of weather or stranding made it almost impossible to obtain cover by any large insurance company. Usually only vessels built under the supervision of a Lloyds surveyor would be considered by them and even then would be at prohibitive cost.

In April 1884 the owners of local ships prudently got together to form their own insurance club. This was known as the Watchet Shipowners' Mutual Assurance Association, but it also accommodated ships from Minehead and Porlock Weir and possibly other ports. Unfortunately no copies of the rules or indeed any documents at all relating to the society are known of by the writer but information handed down by word of mouth implied that each new member on joining paid a fee of 3% of the value of his ship. The value would be decided by the other members and was kept on the low side, and it rarely exceeded £200. Should a member's ship be a total loss all members would then pay an additional levy of 3% of the already agreed value of the ship that was lost. Should a vessel be stranded and thought by its master to be unsalvageable, the society could, and often did send its own assessor to determine if the ship should be considered a total loss or whether salvage attempts should be paid for by the society. The simple system would appear to have worked well for many years. But after the disastrous gale of 1900 which almost destroyed the harbour and many of its ships, as well as further losses in 1901 the Society was in a bad way financially.

According to reports in the *West Somerset Free Press* total claims in excess of £1000 were paid out at this time. Eight Watchet members' vessels had been completely lost or written off plus the *Penguin* of Porlock Weir.

Also in 1901 the ketch *Charlotte* under Capt. Searle had run aground and capsized in the Yougal river in Ireland. The wreck was inspected by Capt. W. Escott on behalf of the Shipowners' Society who considered it would be too costly and risky to warrant salvage attempts by the Shipowners' Society. Capt. J. Davis, the owner, was therefore paid out according to the levy agreement. The wreck of the *Charlotte* was then auctioned by the society and was purchased by her previous owner Capt. Davis who was of the opinion that the vessel could possibly be salvaged. (The salvage attempt on the *Charlotte* will be referred to later).

The Shipowners' Society was still in existence in 1911, for in a local press report of a meeting on February 11 of that year the Hon. Sec. Mr. N. Hole reported that there was a balance in hand of £181. 3. 2d. When they eventually wound up the society is not known but certainly during its existence over many years it was able to provide a little help when it was desperately needed.

The Coastguards

Coastguards have been stationed at Watchet for a very long time and well over a hundred years ago they occupied the very tall houses at the top of Causeway Terrace where they enjoyed a panoramic view of the Bristol Channel.

Daily they patrolled along the beaches or along the cliff top coastguard paths to Blue Anchor or St. Audries Bay. They also had their own boats for patrolling the coast.

On one occasion in the 1870's William Norman (grandfather of the writer) who was on his way to the harbour, was pressed into service, very much against his will by order of the Head Coastguard to help row the coastguards' boat in an abortive attempt to detain and search a small ship reported near the shore in St. Audries Bay.

From 1897 the Coastguards were housed in a block of newly built and

A very early photograph thought to be one of the three original hobble boats. The two uniformed men in the boat are coastguards who, like the ladies, probably couldn't resist posing for a photograph. A most interesting and intriguing character study.

typical Coastguard Cottages at Highbank overlooking the harbour. Here a signal mast was erected, lawns and gardens laid out and everything was kept in immaculate order.

During the 1914/18 war the regular coastguard's staff was greatly depleted, and a number of men over the age of call-up were taken on as coast watchers. Armed with sword sticks, presumably for self-defence, they patrolled the beaches and were on constant watch for enemy submarines.

In the 1930's the regular coastguards were stood down and the cottages were sold.

In the 1939/45 war Coastwatchers were again recruited. The Hobblers' watch house on the West Pier was taken over and an observation tower was erected on the top of it. It was constantly manned, during hostilities, mainly by veteran seamen.

After the lifeboat station closed in 1944 Auxiliary Coastguards were recruited with Mr. John Harris Norman in charge. The Hobblers Watch house was used by them for bad weather watches and later a new observation tower was built on the cliffs above the harbour.

Since 1974 a full time Coastguard Officer has been stationed at Watchet in charge of the Auxiliaries. Constant erosion and difficulty of access caused the cliff top watch tower to be abandoned in December 1981.

The present Coastguard Officer now has a combined Look-out and Office situated on the Esplanade overlooking the harbour and the Channel.
and the Channel.

With a number of Auxiliaries he patrols the Somerset and Devon Coast between Bridgwater and Lee Abbey. The Station is fully equipped with rocket apparatus and lifesaving gear which can speedily be taken anywhere along the coast in the Rescue Landrover. A fast inflatable boat is also at hand to allow coastal patrol when necessary.

WATCHET HARBOURMASTERS: 1809-1985

Year appointed

1809	William Boswell
1838	Peter Boswell
1858	Robert Bussell
1867	Edwin Forde
1880	Robert Board
1883	John Norman
1884	Henry Watts
1903	Alfred Norman
1911	Gowen Hunt
1941	Harry Redd
1953	Thomas Ley
1974	Christoffel Muller

Coastwatchers were appointed in World War I. (Top row, left to right): Ernest Escott, H. Onslow, chief coastguard and James Baker. (Bottom row): Jack Norman, Robert Nicholas, Walter Norman and Jack Strong.

(By courtesy Mrs. J. Norman)

CHAPTER 8

TALES OF WATCHET SHIPS

Watchet's Ship Building Industry

Some shipbuilding was carried on at Watchet mainly during the 1800's. Small vessels were built on a site at Yard Beach which was situated at the eastward side of the harbour. The industry was of necessity terminated when the site was required for the new harbour developed in 1860. The names and particulars of ten vessels built at Watchet were given to the writer by the marine historian, Capt. James Dew of Burnham-on-Sea, as follows:

1788	*Venus*	Sloop 4 tons	Owner, when built, unknown. Owner in 1793 Robert Loue of Bridgwater – Gentleman.	
1815	*Britannia*	Schooner 75 tons	Joint Owners: William Hole – Merchant George Royall – Timber Merchant	
1820	*Watchet Trader* built by George Geen	Sloop 39.2 tons	Owner – Ann Whaddon, Widow of Watchet.	
1824	*Appollo*	Schooner 58 tons	Owners: William House of Bridgwater Joseph Paul of Bridgwater Edmund Westlake of Watchet Elizabeth Hartnoll	Shares 24 16 8 16 = Total Shares: 64
1825	*Ceres*	Smack 37 tons	Owners: William Gimblett James Gimblett Merchants of Watchet	Shares 32 32 = Total Shares: 64
1837	*Friendship*	Schooner 54.4 tons	Owner: Henry Hole of Watchet	Shares: 64
1848	*Margery*	Sloop 26 tons	Owner: William Stoate of Watchet	Shares: 64
1852	*Friends* built by George Geen	Smack 31 tons	Owners: Robert Gimblett John Gimblett (of Watchet)	Shares 32 32 = Total Shares: 64
1858	*Lynn*	Smack 34 tons	Owner: Thomas Geen of Lynmouth (possibly the builder)	

99

1859	*Star of the West* built by George Escott Geen	Schooner 82 tons	Owner: George Escott Geen, Shipbuilder – Watchet	Shares: 64

1863: Sold to new owners:
Albert Williams,
Merchant – Watchet 32
George Taylor,
Doctor – Watchet 16
Samuel Cox,
Bookseller – Williton 16
= Total Shares: 64

1869: Sold to Thomas Martin Davis,
Master Mariner of Watchet ..... Shares: 64

Note – a family of shipwrights named Geen were building ships at Appledore in early 1800's. One wonders whether the Watchet shipwright Geen might have originated from there.

Some Watchet Owned Sailing Ships

Among the largest of Watchet's sailing fleet was the Brig *Princess Royal,* built at Swansea in 1851 and owned by George Passmore. She was lost without trace in 1881 while sailing from Newport to Plymouth. The entire crew of six were lost, including two young brothers: R. & J. Norman, aged 25 and 17, W. Browning, J. Cridland, W. Maxwell and W. Hole (Captain).

A large three-masted schooner was the *Slyboots* (what an intrigueing name) she was built at Dartmouth in 1868 and owned by Henry G. Norman. She ran ashore in fog on the Suffolk coast in 1896 and became a total loss. Her crew of six were saved.

Another three-master was the *Doctor,* built at Burton Stather in 1864 and owned by Henry John Watts and Charles Vicary. In 1892 Captain Charles Vicary, master, had a very narrow escape from being murdered when the cook, a Swansea man, fired a revolver at him in his cabin, the bullet grazing the Captain's head. This happened just after Capt. Vicary had charged the man with stealing money from his cabin. On the eve of Christmas 1894 when under the command of Capt. J. Wilkins, the *Doctor* was caught in a gale in Belfast Lough, and was driven onto a lee shore and wrecked. Three of his crew of five, including two young brothers Milton, were drowned while attempting to reach the shore.

The schooner *Mary Louisa* was built in France in 1849 and was owned while at Watchet by Henry J. Watts and later by John Henry Nicholas.

Ships were often named after people and sometimes people were named after ships. The late Mrs Marie Louise Duddridge of Watchet was named after this French-built vessel, and even the writer, at his father's wish, was named after one of his family's long lost ships, the sloop *William Henry.* His mother, however, disliked this name and persisted in calling him Ben. This name stuck, and was eventually "adopted". The sloop *William Henry* referred to, was of

40 tons Reg., and built at Brixham in 1868. When owned at Watchet by Capt. William Norman, she was one of the small ships which were cut in half and lengthened at nearby Helwell Bay and in 1883 re-rigged as a ketch. In 1887 in Swansea Bay she was again cut in half, but unfortunately this time it was by a steamer, the *S.S. Supernal* of Sunderland, she sank immediately and one man, Samuel Burston was lost.

The Brig *Benjamin Boyd*, 131 tons Reg., voyaged 14000 miles before joining the Watchet fleet. She was built at Manning River in New South Wales in 1844. She was owned there by Benjamin Boyd the founder of the Australian whaling industry in Two Fold Bay. While at Watchet she was owned by Capt. Tom Chidgey and was rigged as a schooner. In 1907 she was cut down in collision with a steamer near Penarth and sank in a few minutes. Captain Chidgey and his crew had barely time to escape with their lives. She was afterwards raised and sold, the new owners eventually filled her with stones and sank her near Penarth where she served the purpose of a small breakwater.

The Aurora

Built at Port Mellon, Cornwall, in 1877 and rigged as fore and aft schooner 34.18 tons reg. she was owned by Henry George Norman of Watchet 1893-1925 and lengthened and altered to ketch rig in 1894. In Dec. 1906 William Henry Norman, the second son of the owner, was master of the *Aurora*. He was found drowned in South Dock, Swansea, and a considerable amount of money he was thought to have upon him was missing. It was thought he was attacked and robbed and thrown into the dock, but the inquest showed no sign of foul play. Another happier tale of the *Aurora* has been handed down. During the 1914-18 war another son was master of the *Aurora*, he was Sydney Norman (no relation of the writer). He found difficulty in finding a crew as many of the local sailors had been called up for war service. As his livelihood depended on taking his ship to sea he in desperation called on his wife to help him. A well built woman and of great courage, she readily agreed to sail with him, and Sydney and his wife alone crewed the *Aurora*. They lived aboard and traded all around the coast throughout the duration of the war and for some years after. Several old sailors confirmed this story and spoke admiringly of her ability to tackle any job that required to be done aboard ship, including going aloft when necessary to set or take in the topsail, taking a turn at the helm or trimming cargo. One of them recalled that when Sydney got involved in a brawl with some foreign sailors at Cardiff, his wife joined in the fray and acquitted herself very well. The late Mrs. Marie Duddridge of Watchet remembered Mrs. Norman and she surprisingly told the writer that the "Mate" of the *Aurora* was a very attractive and good-looking woman and when she stepped ashore, she was always "Dressed up like a chocolate box"?

Mr. Dick Norman, a distant relative of Captain Sydney believes that either

The ketch "Aurora" which was crewed by Capt. Norman and his wife.
(Original painting by Thos. Chidgey)

a badge, medal or a diploma was awarded to Mrs. Norman in recognition of her war service, but the writer after many enquiries, is unable to ascertain if this was so. By all accounts she certainly deserved one.

The Kings Oak

The *Kings Oak* was considered by many Watchet sailors to be a very fast sailing vessel. According to Capt. Jim Dew's record of Watchet ships, she was built at Southtown, Yarmouth in 1884 by J. H. Fellows & Sons and launched in August as a sailing trawler. In 1891 she was lengthened at Bridgwater and re-rigged as a fore and aft schooner, and from that date was owned by Spillers and Bakers, millers of Cardiff. From 1901 until 1923 she was owned by Capt. Richard Harris of Watchet and in 1916 the *Kings Oak* is on record as having sailed from Waterford to Bridgwater 250 miles in thirty hours (a record at that time.) The *Kings Oak* having originally been built as a sailing trawler was of deep draught and this probably accounted for her fast sailing capabilities, particularly when sailing to windward.

Her sharp bottom however was a nuisance in Watchet's tidal harbour for it allowed her to heel over acutely when she grounded. For this reason Captain Harris preferred trading from Bridgwater where his ship could always lie afloat in the dock.

A Watchet veteran, Mr. Ernest Binding, who is over ninety years old, can remember his father, a master mariner, and numerous other Watchet sailors standing on the pier at Watchet and gazing out to sea, some armed with binoculars and telescopes. A smart new ketch had been built at Bridgwater and was due to sail from that port to Ireland. Her name was the *Irene* and she was the last ship to be built there in 1907. It appeared that the *Irene* and the *Kings Oak* under the command of Captain Harris were to leave Bridgwater on the same tide and were both bound for the same port in Ireland with bricks. Wagers had been laid by Watchet and Bridgwater men as to which was the fastest ship. Mr. Binding said that when both ships passed down channel abreast of Watchet the sailors were chuckling happily as the *Kings Oak* was well in the lead.

In Jan. 1911 while on voyage from Liverpool for Bridgwater, the *Kings Oak* encountered heavy weather, and Captain Harris had the traumatic experience of seeing his son Tom washed overboard and lost. Old sailors recalled that when the *Kings Oak* was next at Watchet she had a blue band painted along her side, this being the usual way of showing a ship was in mourning. One of the crew of the *Kings Oak* remembered by Mr. Binding and the writer was the late Tom Cridland who would recite little jingles about the weather etc. One that comes to mind was as follows:—

> When the sun goes down behind a bank,
> Westerly Winds you will have to thank,
> When the sun goes down as clear as a bell,
> Easterly Winds will blow like hell.

Mr. Cridland served in the Merchant Navy during the second World War until well past retirement age. He was awarded the B.E.M.

Incidentally the *Irene* outlasted the entire British fleet of small sailing coasters and continued to trade until 1961. She is still afloat and has been completely re-rigged as original. In August 1983 her owner and master Leslie Morrish brought her into Watchet Harbour and the public were allowed aboard. Donations were taken in aid of the R.N.L.I. funds. (See illustration of *Irene* on back cover.)

The Louise

Built at Gannel Yard, Newquay 1877 by Richard Chegwidden 114 gross tons, 99 nett. The *Louise,* a fine top sail schooner, was owned by Thomas Chidgey, Watchet's marine artist and crewed by his three sons Robert, Thomas and George. Robert who was master and a part share holder, once told the writer of an experience when the *Louise* was caught in a gale of wind while at anchor in Penarth Roads. The wind had changed in direction from Westerly to East North East and what had been a sheltered anchorage was now open to the full fury of an on shore gale. Both anchors had been out and one had parted its cable, the other started dragging. The *Louise* and all aboard were in great danger. The only hope of survival was to get some sail on the vessel, slip

The Fore & Aft Schooner "Kings Oak," a painting by Reuben Chappel.
(By courtesy Mrs. N. Gilks)

Captain Richard Harris aboard the "Kings Oak." On his left is his son Tom
who was washed overboard and drowned. Thomas Cridland is on the right.
(By courtesy Mrs. N. Gilks)

the remaining anchor and hope to clear the headland of Lavernock Point. This was done and the headland was just cleared. They then ran down channel and away to the open sea. Had they had more anchors aboard, they might have sought shelter in some haven or bay. A sailing ship without an anchor would not normally enter a harbour even in a moderate breeze. In a gale of wind it would probably be disastrous, and so they had to run to the open sea for safety. The *Louise* was a well found and able vessel and with careful handling she survived the gale which lasted for several days. When the weather eventually moderated, the Chidgey brothers tired and hungry, brought the *Louise* back to Barry Roads where they hailed a tug and negotiated a tow into port. The anchors were subsequently salvaged and returned to the *Louise*. Captain Bob said that several ships were driven ashore during the same gale and lives were lost. (See illustration of *Louise* on front cover.)

The Taunton Packet

The *Taunton Packet* 74.9 tons reg. was built at Bridgwater in 1838 by Watson, Luer & Co. and rigged as a two mast schooner; from 1881-1883 she was owned by J. L. Kingsbury of Watchet. In Feb. 1883 the vessel foundered in a storm off the Bishops Lighthouse, near the Scillies and the crew took to the boat. Their ordeal is graphically described in a letter which the survivers, Robert Wedlake (Master), Alfred Pittaway (Mate) and W. Morgan (AB) wrote to the editor of the *West Somerset Free Press* (letter as follows):

"We the undersigned, are the shipwrecked crew of the *Taunton Packet* of Watchet, which foundered off the Bishops on Friday, the 2nd inst., at four o'clock p.m., but through a merciful providence our lives were spared, having taken to the boat, which we were in for fifteen hours, in a fearful gale of wind, accompanied by snow and hail. We had a crew of four all told, but the carpenter, Amos Sutton of Minehead, died whilst in the boat, through exposure, after twelve hours pulling. At last we reached a creek, Goodwick, in Fishguard Bay, at 7.30 a.m. on Saturday, the 3rd when we received the greatest kindness from the inhabitants. We were at once clothed by Capt. Bowen and Capt. George, and lodgings were procured as well; and not thinking this enough, they very kindly made a collection for us amongst the inhabitants, and a collection was also made in each chapel and church to give us. We were thoroughly exhausted, having had nothing to eat for forty-eight hours; in fact we could not have held out much longer. As it was, we were frost-bitten and almost done for. The carpenter, Amos Sutton, was buried in a most respectable manner by the inhabitants in a coffin covered with black cloth and suitable appendages. His body was buried at Llanarn, followed by the gentry and inhabitants. We think it right publicly to thank the friends of this place for their very great kindness, and shall feel obliged if you will do so through your widely circulated paper."

105

The Kelso

Basil Greenhill and Ann Gifford in their book "West Country Men in Prince Edward Isle" reveal that during the 1800's, many Westcountryfolk including a number of shipwrights emigrated to Prince Edward Island, near Newfoundland. With plenty of mature timber available they set to work building ships, many of which were then sailed back to this country and sold. Some of these ships eventually came to join the Watchet fleet. They include:

The Cardigan	owned by John Wilkinson Redd	1892-1903
The Princess	owned by Benjamin Williams	1869-1887
The Henrietta	owned by Francis Norman (father of the writer)	1904-1907

Another of these ships was the *Kelso*, a lovely looking schooner of 68 tons reg. and built in 1866 at Souris by John Douse. The following strange tales of this ship have often been told at Watchet:—

The *Kelso* was purchased in 1868 by John and William Besley, ropemakers and fishermen of Watchet, and was for a time, under the command of Capt. Joe Pittaway who had previously spent some time in the Newfoundland cod trade. By the 1880's she had come under the command of Capt. William

Captain Joseph Pittaway who traded to Newfoundland and for a time was master of the "Kelso." *(By courtesy Mrs. W. Bryant)*

106

Webber and was trading frequently to Ireland. On one occasion he took his eight year old son with him and at Waterford he gave the little lad a linnet in a cage.

On Friday the 26th January 1883 while returning from Ireland in ballast, the *Kelso* ran into a terrific storm in the Bristol Channel. She capsized and was lost. That evening the brig *Pioneer* sighted the nearly submerged hull and just managed to read the *Kelso's* name on the stern. Being under stress of weather, she was unable to report this information for some time.

Meanwhile, at their little terraced house at Watchet, Capt. Webber's wife and little son heard the whining of the wind. The *Kelso* was expected and Dad was in their thoughts. Mrs. Webber was in the small kitchen preparing a meal. The boy was sitting beside the fire in the living-room. Suddenly he jumped up, he had distinctly seen his father at the window complete with his sailor's kit bag and heard him tapping on the window. The boy ran to his mother calling that Dad was home. His mother had also heard the tapping and they both hurried to open the door .... Until his dying day the boy was convinced he had seen his father at the window, his mother believed him and was certain she had also heard the tapping on the window. No-one has ever been able to explain the mystery of the little lad's vision of his father, probably no-one ever will. It is perhaps best summed up by the old saying that goes "There are more things in Heaven and Earth etc. ...".

Another strange but authentic story of this same disaster has also been handed down amongst Watchet's seafaring families. The *Kelso* having not arrived back in port when expected, was some days overdue. The harbour community was apprehensive and feared for her safety as they were aware that she must have encountered severe weather. Their fears were confirmed in a remarkable way.

The brothers John and William Besley, owners of the *Kelso,* were also fishermen, and while fishing with nets off Watchet, the nets became tangled with some wreckage. This they immediately recognised as part of a jib-boom from the *Kelso*. It bore the marks of a repair that had recently been carried out. They knew then for sure that the *Kelso* would never return.

The crew lost on the *Kelso* were:
William Webber – master; Robert Searle – mate; Albert Strickland – A.B.; James Bale – boy.

The Charlotte

Built at Southampton in 1867 by C. Langley, 73 ton reg., rigged as a ketch and owned at Watchet 1892 until 1927.

In May 1901 the *Charlotte* was owned by Capt. Thomas Davis of Watchet. Captain Searle, master, had taken her to Janeville, eleven miles up the Blackwater river in Ireland where she loaded a cargo of oats consigned for Swansea. Before sailing up the river Capt. Searle had waited a considerable time at

107

Yougal for a pilot. Eventually he had to go without one and worked his way up river with the assistance of a "River Man". The same difficulty arose in coming down river. No pilot was available and ominously, no river man would come to advise.

After waiting several days Captain Searle decided to try to get his ship down river unaided. As there was no wind it was decided to tow the *Charlotte* down river on the ebb tide using the vessel's own boat, rowed by the crew. All went well until abreast of Crineen Reach when a strong set of tide carried the *Charlotte* toward the Eastern bank. The anchor was let go, but there was not enough room to swing, and the keel of the vessel struck a submerged rocky ledge. In this position the *Charlotte* remained fast despite every effort of the crew to shift her. As the tide ebbed she gradually toppled on to her side, her masts parallel with the water. Her cargo swelled, bursting from her hatches and a large part of her cargo of oats floated down stream. She remained on her side with only her bilge visible. After some days the Captain and crew were sent home by the Shipwrecked Mariners' Society of Youghal.

Capt. Davis, the owner, and Capt. Frank Norman (father of the writer) took some gear to Ireland hoping to enable the *Charlotte* to be salvaged. Before this could be done it was essential to hire a barge, but this proved at first to be impossible. Although there were dozens of barges laying unused

Captain Frank Norman (father of the author) who took command of the schooners "Thomas Aylan", "Henrietta", "Tankerton Tower", and the ketch "Charlotte".

along the river, not one could be spared even though generous payment was offered. It was obvious to Capt. Norman that the rivermen were waiting for the salvage attempts to be abandoned. They, the rivermen, would then salvage the ship themselves. Captain Norman went to Youghal where he knew a friendly master of an Irish vessel, and asked for his help. The Irish Captain said it would be more than his life was worth to come himself or to be seen to interfere by the rivermen who were a law unto themselves. But he gave some Irish advice.

A generous donation to the Parish Priest *'for Church funds'* might, he thought, prove helpful in producing a barge. This was done. The Priest was told of the problem and he accepted the donation which was handed over with some misgivings. He could promise nothing, he said, but if it were God's will then a barge might possibly be forthcoming in due course. The very next day a barge miraculously became available but at a non miraculous price. It was placed in position at low water under the mast of the *Charlotte,* still on her side. As the tide rose the barge lifted the mast and with the aid of blocks and tackle, sheerlegs, and an anchor dug in ashore, the *Charlotte,* as the tide fell, was pulled upright. She had received comparatively little damage and she returned to Watchet.

A few months after the mishap, the *Charlotte* under the command of Capt. Norman lost almost every stitch of canvas in heavy weather off the South East coast of Ireland and had to be assisted into Kinsale.

In April 1916 a blizzard of great suddenness and fury drove the *Charlotte* ashore at Blue Anchor near Watchet. The rigging was coated with ice and the decks were like glass. Captain Frank Norman and his crew clung to the rigging during the night. The *Charlotte* was eventually left high and dry by the ebbing tide and the men made their way through deep snow drifts to Watchet on foot. The ketch was later refloated and again returned to trade from Watchet mainly with coal for the paper mills. In 1927 the *Charlotte* was broken up at the West Pier and her keelson, spars, deck beams and hatches were used in the construction of a large shed in the mineral yard. This shed was used as a garage for the Lavender Blue buses, the first to operate from Watchet.
For some years it was used by Watchet Boat Owners' for repairs, but in 1990 it was washed away by the sea in a violent storm.

The Naiad

Built of lome iron at Llanelly in 1864, the *Naiad* was considered by many to be Watchet's finest topsail schooner. Of 149 tons gross, 121 nett, she was built and owned until 1902 by C. Nevill of Llanelly. For some time she carried cargoes of wine from Sicily and was said to have taken some cargoes to New York.

In 1902 she was purchased by:

Steve Allen of Watchet	16 shares
Albert Allen of Watchet	16 shares

William Robert Allan of Watchet . . . . 16 shares
Henry Smith of Charlestown, Cornwall . . . . 16 shares

She was engaged in the general coasting trade. Captain Harry Redd of Watchet (Master).

During the 1914/18 war the *Naiad* was fitted with a gun as a defence against possible attack by submarines and a couple of Naval gunners were carried to man the gun. They were given nicknames while at Watchet and were known affectionately as "Mutt" and "Geoff" (characters from a comic strip). The gun had never fired a shot since being fitted but on one hazy, almost windless day while some way off the coast in the English Channel the gunners who were inclined to boast and brag of their accurate marksmanship were taunted by the crew of the *Naiad* and mischievously cast doubts on their ability to hit a floating haystack, much less a submarine. The gunners eventually persuaded Captain Redd to let them fire just one shot to prove their ability and bets were laid with the doubting crew.

An old wooden box was heaved overboard to act as a target and after it had drifted quite a way off a shot was fired. The box was not hit much to the delight of the *Naiad's* crew, but much to the annoyance of Capt. Harry the vibration broke the glass in the cabin skylight. The noise of the gun

Captain Harry Redd (right) Master of the schooner "Naiad" and Captain Steven Allen, part owner. Captain Redd was later to be Harbourmaster at Watchet.   *(By courtesy Michael Bouquet)*

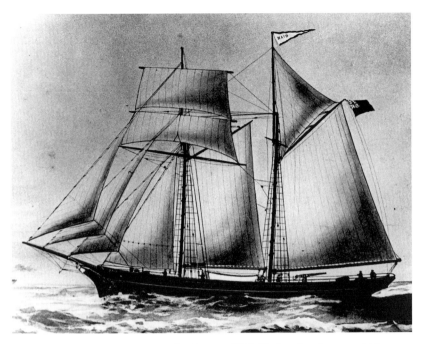

A picture of the iron topsail schooner "Naiad" showing the gun which was fired by "Mutt & Geoff". *(By courtesy John Gilman)*

The "Naiad" the last of Watchet's sailing fleet on the rocks of Looe in 1931. She had dragged ashore in a gale of wind and was a total loss.

however, had been heard ashore, and before long a small naval patrol boat came rushing out "with a bone in her teeth" (i.e. foaming at the bow). Mutt and Jeff were apprehensive and at a loss for words of explanation. 'Leave it to me to do the talking', said Capt. Harry and in due course he explained to the officers on the patrol vessel that he had ordered the gun to be fired at what in the haze looked like the conning tower of an enemy submarine. Just at that moment the look-out on the patrol vessel let out a yell for he had just spotted the box floating in the far distance. Capt. Harry said nothing, and the patrol vessel hurried off to investigate and did not come back. Many years later Capt. Harry laughingly told the writer that he often wondered what the Officer in command wrote in his official report.

In March 1931 the *Naiad* was anchored and waiting for the tide off Looe. She was loaded with 100 tons of granite blocks. A sudden gale sprang up and she dragged ashore. With great difficulty the crew was taken off by the pilot Capt. Taums and his son in the pilot boat, but the lovely *Naiad* was a total loss. She was the last of Watchet's sailing fleet.

The Cimbri

The powerful three masted schooner *Cimbri* 150 tons was built by Westacotts of Barnstaple in 1877. This ship was copper fastened and her bottom sheathed with yellow metal to resist wood boring Toredo worms (quite common in foreign waters).

The *Cimbri* had spent some years in the Newfoundland cod trade and had been owned at Gloucester before coming into the ownership of the Allen family of Watchet in 1885. Because of the slackening of trade at Watchet due to the closure of the iron ore mines, the *Cimbri* at this time, sailed mainly from Charlestown in Cornwall with cargoes of china clay. She was under the command of Henry Smith, a Watchet sea captain who had moved to Charlestown and taken up residence there. He took 16 shares in the *Cimbri* and eventually bought her outright.

The writer's father was related to Capt. Smith and as a youth he also moved to Charlestown to train under Captain Henry aboard the *Cimbri*. The writer possesses a tattered discharge certificate and wages account signed by Capt. Smith in 1896. It records that seaman Frank Norman, aged 20, was discharged at Newport after a voyage in the *Cimbri* to Antwerp and Cincarneau. His ability and conduct was recorded as very good and his wages for a month were £3. 5. 0.

The *Cimbri* was eventually wrecked in 1924.

Another Watchet man who also moved to Charlestown to live was Capt. Frank Larcombe. Among several ships which he commanded was the Fowey built topsail schooner *Thomas Aylan,* also owned by the Allen family of Watchet. This fine schooner was in 1902 under the command of the aforementioned Frank Norman. Among old papers recently discovered under the

paper lining of Capt. Norman's old sea chest was a butcher's receipt dated
Nov. 17, 1902 for 18lbs. of beef 9/- and 1lb of suet 6d. delivered to the
schooner *Thomas Aylen* from a butcher s shop near Liverpool.

A very quick voyage must have followed this purchase for also in the
chest was another receipt dated Nov. 18, 1902. It was for *Thomas Aylan*
pilotage dues 8/- paid to Cork Harbour Commissioners. Other schooners
later to come under Cap'n Norman's command were the *Tankerton Tower*
and the *Henrietta.*

The Trio

The *Trio* was built in Jersey in 1876, a very smart little topsail schooner.
She was employed in the Newfoundland cod trade before coming to Watchet
in 1895. The *Trio* was one of several schooners owned by the Escott family.
In 1909 she was sold to the Slade family of Appledore who re-rigged her as a
ketch. From 1919 until 1939 she was owned by Joseph Warren, master
mariner of Bridgwater, who fitted her with an auxiliary engine. Her end
came in 1939 when she slipped off her berth on the steep sides of the River
Parrett and fell on her side. On the next tide she filled and opened up. She
became a total loss and her hull was blown up.

The Bonita and the Democrat

The very last sailing vessel to enter and leave Watchet harbour under sail
alone in June 1934 was the *Bonita,* a small ketch from Braunton, near
Barnstaple, Reuben Chichester, owner and master.

The ketch "Bonita" at Watchet, 1930's. The man balanced on the foot-
ropes under the bowsprit is adjusting the bobstay.

The writer remembers with affection this grand old sailor who despite being crippled after a fall from aloft, continued to sail his little craft, with one other crew member (usually his son).

Reuben always carried a violin aboard ship and being a strict teetotaller he occasionally took his fiddle to entertain the "Band of Hope", a temperance organisation which was attached to the Methodist church situated near the harbour. Here, after playing a tune or two, Reuben advised the youth of the town (including the writer) to abstain from intoxicating liquor. Some (alas) heeded not the Captain's words and in later years succumbed to temptation. He spoke with great sincerity, for as a boy he had seen his own father drown in Swansea dock due to a drinking session.

The *Bonita* was of only sixty tons burthen and freights for such a little ship at the time were very difficult to come by. Her last cargoes at Watchet were of coal for the West Somerset Coal and Trading Co. Reuben and his son barely earned a living. In August 1934, the *Bonita* was driven ashore in a gale of wind at Aberthaw and her bottom was ripped out on the rocks. When the tide had receded and left her high and dry on the rocks, Capt. Reuben was seen by watchers on shore to leave his doomed ship and hobble ashore carrying his beloved fiddle.

Capt. Reuben later took command of the *Democrat,* a very smart ketch, which had been fitted with an oil engine albiet a temperamental one. As a youth, the writer sailed with him on the *Democrat* to Lydney and remembers that after sailing for a while the wind died away and the *Democrat* proceeded up Channel under power of the engine alone. When in the fast flowing tidal River Severn, well below Lydney, the engine spluttered to a stop. Captain Reuben was prepared for such an emergency for he let go a long chain which he had got ready. This was allowed to drag along the bottom of the river.

By putting the helm hard over he was able to cant the head of the vessel so that she sheered towards the chosen shore as she drifted along with the fast flowing tide. Capt. Reuben declined the immediate offer of a tow by a passing small and ugly looking little steamer called the *Black Dwarf* but he craftily requested her skipper to hang about just in case. When almost off Lydney fortunately the engine which had been furiously worked on and soundly cursed by Reuben's son burst into life and, after hauling in the chain, the *Democrat* was able to enter the already open lock gates.

Capt. Reuben later explained that his previous little ketch the *Bonita* having no engine was entirely dependent on the force of the wind, or tidal or river currents, therefore he on many occasions had to work his way up or down a river or estuary by the dragging chain method. Sometimes he said the ship's anchor would be lowered and allowed to just touch bottom as it dragged along, but he preferred using a chain as it was less likely to get caught up. Aboard the *Bonita* he also carried a pair of large oars or sweeps which on windless days were used to laboriously move the little vessel perhaps into mid stream or away from a quayside.

114

Reuben's son who did the cooking aboard ship almost daily produced his speciality, a "Tiddy Oggy", a sort of Cornish Pasty with plenty of vegetables and very little meat.

After Reuben retired, the *Democrat* was still active in the Bristol Channel under Captain Coates also of Braunton and was one of the last ketches to trade in the Channel.

WATCHET'S STEAM SHIPS

The Rushlight

Built at Greenock by Ross and Marshall in 1902, 118 tons gross, 56 nett.

This little Clyde Puffer puffed in and out of Watchet harbour for over 40 years. The *Rushlight* came to Watchet in 1910 having been purchased by the Wansborough Paper Co. for £1,600. Captain W.J.Norman with a Watchet crew brought her from Troon in Scotland and except for a period during the first world war when she was a tender to the Grand Fleet at Scapa Flow, she traded regularly from Watchet until 1953.

Captain Norman made over 3000 trips in her, mainly bringing culm from Welsh ports to feed the boilers of the paper mills. He was succeeded by Capt. Jack Allen in 1947.

A notable member of the crew was Mr. Dick Hill who was the engineer cum stoker for over twenty years. The engine room was so cramped that Dick had to cut six inches off a normal sized shovel in order to fire the boiler. The *Rushlight's* cargo was always of very dusty small coal (culm). Not surprisingly some of the crew who always had to trim the cargo with shovels would swallow a lot of dust and on reaching Watchet would often hasten to the nearest pub to wash it down with beer. Here they would almost certainly meet up with sailors from other ships on a similar mission. One crew member in particular required rather a lot of beer to clear the dust and according to his wife stayed for too long in the pub. On several occasions she hauled him out, and once remarked in exasperation: "My husband can't go into a pub and drink thirteen or fourteen pints like a normal man and then come home, he's got to stay in the pub until he's had a ! * ! gutsfull."

The *Rushlight* was broken up at Llannelly in 1953. A scale model of this little ship made by Mr. G. Neale is on view at the Watchet museum.

The Radstock

The *Radstock* reg. Bridgwater 111395. Built at Saltney Chester in 1925 by J. Crichton & Co. Ltd., 195 tons gross, 78 nett, for the Somerset and Dorset Railway Co. and operated mainly from Highbridge. The smart little steamship was owned and commanded for many years by Capt. W. Morse of Watchet. During the 1930 s the *Radstock* was chartered by the R.A.F. and used by them at Watchet to recover radio controlled aeroplanes known as Queen Bees which were being used for practice by a nearby Anti-Aircraft Gunnery

Brigade. The pilotless planes which were fitted with floats, were catapulted into the air and if not shot down would alight on the sea and be brought back to harbour by the *Radstock*. During the second world war she tended the Navy at Portsmouth.

St. Decumans

Reg. Bridgwater 68145. Built at Bridgwater in 1873 by John Gough. Carvel built of wood. 134 tons gross, 81 nett. This was probably the first steam ship to trade regularly from Watchet. She was specially built to carry iron ore and was owned by James Ware of Cardiff until sold in 1895. From 1910-23 with her engine removed, she was in use at Liverpool as a coal barge.

Dunster Castle

Reg. Liverpool 128012, built at Garston in 1909 by Garston C.D. and S.B. Co. Ltd. 155 tons gross, 62 nett.

The *Dunster Castle* traded from Watchet, Minehead, Bristol and other small ports with small amounts of general cargo in competition with the dwindling fleet of ketches and smacks. She was commanded by Capt. Thomas Allen of Watchet from 1909-1911 and was owned by West Somerset & Bristol Channel Steam Ship Co., Liverpool. Whereas the Brig *Benjamin Boyd* voyaged 14000 miles from Australia eventually to trade from Watchet, the *Dunster Castle* made the same voyage in reverse. From 1917 until 1953 she was registered and trading from Melbourne, Australia.

The Karrier

This little steam ship was not at Watchet for long. Built at Sorel in Canada in 1917, she was owned by a local syndicate known as the Watchet Trading Co. who used her to carry local farm produce and general cargo mainly to the Welsh ports and return with cargoes of coal. Capt. William Morse was Master. A tragedy occurred soon after her purchase in Scotland. The engineer, Harry Norman, had gone inside the boiler to carry out an inspection when he was overcome by fumes. Despite heroic efforts by William Webber and others, who eventually at great risk to their own lives, got him out of the boiler, he was found to be dead.

As before mentioned the Trading Co. built a huge warehouse on the edge of the Quay, and in August 1924 the warehouse with a large section of the wharf had collapsed into the harbour. The *Karrier* laying alongside the wharf at the time was damaged. Soon after this calamity the Company ceased trading and the *Karrier* left Watchet.

The Arran Monarch

The *Arran Monarch* reg. London 180868, built at Faversham 1946 by J. Pollack Sons & Co., 147 tons gross, 52 nett, owned by Wansborough Paper Co She succeeded the veteran *Rushlight* in 1953 bringing culm for use in the steam boilers at the local paper mills. When new oil burning boilers were installed at the paper mill in 1963 she was surplus to requirements and was sold to Mr. Peter Herbert of Bude. She was lengthened, re-engined and converted into a sand sucker and was renamed the *Coedmor*. She was the last of the Watchet owned steam ships.

The *Coedmor* is at present active at Wadebridge in Cornwall.

A list of Watchet-owned sailing ships compiled by Mr. A. B. L. Pearse and presented to Watchet Urban District Council in 1934:

Name	Rig.	Ton'ge	Owner
Ann (Bonny Brown)	Ketch	100	J. G. Passmore
Annie Jones	Schooner	180	Hy. Norman
Astrea	Schooner	190	H. Organ
Alpha	Schooner	160	R. Norman
Alpha	Schooner	250	J. Watts
Annie Christian	Fore-&-Aft Schooner	130	J. Allen
Abeona	Smack	28	R. Wedlake
Albert	Ketch	80	A. Nicholas
Alfreda	Schooner	220	A. Allen
Aurora	Fore-&-Aft Schooner	60	H. Norman
* Ark	Yacht	10	B. Williams
Blue Bell	Ketch	100	Norman
Branch	Schooner	200	Norman
Benjamin Boyd	Schooner	180	T. Chidgey
Betsy	Smack	50	Williams
Charles Phillips	Smack	50	R. Case
Coronella	Schooner	150	J. Allen
Commodore	Smack	50	Nicholas
Charles Tucker	Schooner	170	Escott
Christabel	Schooner	200	Passmore
Charlotte	Ketch	140	Davis
Cardigan	Schooner	140	Redd
Caroline	Brigantine	280	Press
Countess of Caithness	Schooner	130	Davis
Curlew	Smack	30	Williams
Cambria	Schooner	240	Allen
Ceres	Smack	70	Allen
Dantzic	Schooner	180	Escott
Dashwood	Schooner	200	Allen
Doctor	3-mast Schooner	300	Vickery
Dewi Winn	Schooner	110	Davis

117

Name	Rig.	Ton'ge	Owner
Electric	Ketch	90	Stoate
Echo	Smack	60	Norman
Express	Ketch	70	Stoate
Elizabeth Hill	Schooner	100	Bruford
Edward & Arthur	3-mast Schooner	280	Norman
Friends	Ketch	80	Thorne
Friends (Little)	Ketch	75	Hole
Fortitude	Smack	80	Allen
Forest Deer	Schooner	130	Allen
Florrie	Smack	70	Chidgey
Fairy King	Schooner	200	Allen
Frederick William	Schooner	100	Rowe
Friendship	Schooner	100	H. Hole
Grimaldi	Schooner	220	Harris
George May	Ketch	70	Norman
Gannet	Ketch	70	Hole
George Canning	Fore-&-Aft Schooner	100	Wedlake
Ginevra	Smack	60	J. Norman
Helen	Schooner	120	Allen
Hawk	Schooner	110	Davis
Harriett Ann	Smack	30	Kingsbury
Heather Bell	Schooner	100	Allen
Hematite	Fore-&-Aft Schooner	180	Vickery
Henrietta	Schooner	120	F. Norman
Helen Tregenzie	Schooner	240	Allen
Jane (Little)	Ketch	70	Norman
John	Schooner	80	Johnson
John George	Smack	65	Kingsbury
J.W.V.	Schooner	120	Norman
J.K.A.	Schooner	120	Escott
Josephine and Marie	Schooner	140	Besley
John Ewin	Schooner	160	Norman
Kelso	Schooner	120	Besley
King's Oak	Ketch	100	Harris
* Lily Green	Trawler	10	Besley
Louise	Ketch	110	Chidgey
Louisa	Schooner	190	Chidgey
Laurina	Smack	28	Wedlake
Lizzie	Ketch	100	Nicholas
Lloyd	Smack	40	Wedlake
Looe	Smack	70	Bryant
Merchant	Smack	50	Merchant
Mizpah	Ketch	120	Allen
Mary Ann	Smack	30	Wedlake
Mary Lauder	Smack	60	Norman
Matford	Schooner	160	J. Lee
Martin Luther	Ketch	80	Nicholas
Minerva	Ketch	160	Griffith
Mary Louisa	Ketch	100	Nicholas
Marjory	Smack	60	Stoate

Name	Rig.	Ton'ge	Owner
Myrtle	Schooner	100	Wedlake
Malfilatre	Brigantine	180	Passmore
Martha	Schooner	160	Davis
Moderator	Smack	80	Kingsbury
Marion	Schooner	180	Escott
Madora	Schooner	80	R. S. Date
Nikita	Schooner	190	Allen
Naiad	Schooner	240	Allen
Ocean	Smack	80	Hole
Providence	Polacca	130	Griffith
Prudence	Schooner	70	Greenslade
Plymouth	Schooner	120	Browning
Princess Royal	Brig	250	Passmore
Princess	Schooner	130	Williams
Pioneer	Smack	50	Binding
Parana	Ketch	90	Vickery
Quiver	Smack	50	Stoate
Queen of the Sea	Schooner	200	Short
Rapid	Schooner	190	Nicholas
Richard	Smack	70	Short
Ruby	Schooner	200	Norman
Rosebud	Smack	60	Kingsbury
Standard	Smack	70	Nicholas
Sprightly	Smack	60	Vickery
St. Catherine	Schooner	120	Watts
Slyboots	3-mast Schooner	170	Norman
* Star of the West	Schooner	140	Davis
Sisters	Schooner	150	Griffith
Trial	Schooner	90	Prosser
Tom	Smack	40	Thorne
Telegraph	Ketch	70	Stoate
Thomas Aylan	Schooner	200	Allen
Trio	Schooner	120	Escott
Thomasine and Mary	Ketch	70	Hole
Taunton	Smack	100	Allen
Taunton Packet	Schooner	120	Kingsbury
Tartar	Smack	70	Wedlake
Thomas and Sarah	Smack	70	Allen
United Friends	Smack	70	Norman
Union	Schooner	110	Short
Union Packet	Smack	70	Gimblett
Venus	Schooner	150	Bruford
Venus	Brigantine	280	Passmore
Welsh Girl	Schooner	220	Morse
William Henry	Ketch	70	Norman

* Built at Watchet

119

CHAPTER 9

THE SMALL FISHING INDUSTRY AND THE STORY OF THE LIFEBOAT

Fishing

Fishing was an early industry at Watchet. Old documents mention salmon fishing, and even to this day the foundations of fishing weirs can be traced on the foreshore off the harbour. The weirs can best be explained as V-shaped walls of loose stones intertwined with saplings and withies. Fish swimming into the open end of the V on the ebb tide would be trapped and left high and dry as the tide receded. Later the introduction of nets which were hung on wooden stakes made them obsolete.

An official report to the Admiralty re Watchet's shipping and fishing industry in 1847 reveals that twenty men were engaged in the local fishing industry and they used ten flat boats for stake net fishing.

The fishing boats used at Watchet were of a very unusual type. Almost flat bottomed with a sharply pointed overhanging bow and stern, they closely resembled the boats known as Dories which were operated from cod fishing schooners on the Newfoundland Grand Banks.

Apart from the Bridgwater river which is the next shipping haven along the coast from Watchet this type of boat was not used for seafishing anywhere around the coast of Britain. This information was given to the writer by the late Harold Kimber, a boat and yacht builder of Highbridge, who also said that similar craft could be found in use only in Scandinavia, Brittany, Portugal and Canada.

The Dories used by the Newfoundland fishing schooners he said were of French origin and built to fit one inside the other when on board ship. Harold and the writer both pondered on the possibility that the local fishing family named Besley who were of French Huguenot descent, might have introduced them to this part of the Somerset coast and demonstrated them to be the most suitable type of craft for the conditions on this difficult stretch of shore.

The boats of Watchet were always referred to as Flatties and at Bridgwater as Flatners, but they were identical in size and shape, approx. 19 ft in length by 5 ft 6 ins beam. Some had a centreboard drop keel and were rigged with an old fashioned type of spritsail. The oars used were also unusual, having square shafts instead of the normal round and each boat was equipped with a wooden

120

Photograph of Boatbuilder, Harold Kimber, standing beside a "Bridgwater Flatner" which he had restored for exhibition at Bristol Museum – c. 1950's. This boat is identical to the "Watchet Flatties" which were used by the Besley family for fishing and is now on display at Watchet Boat Museum.

Stake net fishing for sprats on the foreshore.

bailer shaped like a small shovel and carved from one piece of wood. Originally Watchet's flatties were built at Watchet but the last ones to be used were built at Combwitch on the Bridgwater river.

Miles of long lines were laid with these boats. Cod, skate, ling, dog fish and conger being the main species caught. Drifting for herring was also carried out during the late autumn and early winter. Quite a lot of fishing was also done from the foreshore which at Watchet dries out for a considerable distance. Rows of wooden stakes were driven into the ground near the low water mark and nets set between them. The fast flowing and ebbing tide would drive fish into the nets which could then be taken from them at the next low water period and carried ashore by horse and cart.

The Besleys who were the major fishing family found that nets set on stakes situated just outside the low water mark were much more prolific than those set inside but boats were needed, both for driving the stakes and for fishing the nets, and their Dory-like flat boats were used for this purpose. The nets set on these outer stakes had iron rings fitted on the bottom corner of each net to allow them to slide down over the stakes.

As much of this type of fishing was done at low water, the Flatties were not usually kept in the harbour but were moored about 200 yards to the North East and outside of the harbour entrance. Some boats were also kept by the Besleys two miles along the shore at Doniford where they had a boathouse at a spot called Lily Green now part of a large holiday complex.

A list of Watchet owned ships collected by the late A. B. L. Pearce includes the *Lily Green,* a ten ton trawler built for the Besleys of Watchet. Unfortunately no date when built or other information has turned up about the little vessel. Besides carrying on the main fishing industry at Watchet, the Besley family were manufacturers of ropes, twines and nets. Their ropemaking machinery and huge cauldrons which were used for tarring the ropes were still in use at the Doniford Road Rope Walk until the early 1930 s. There were also other cauldrons used for boiling the bark of oak trees, the resulting brew was used on canvas sails and fishing nets to prevent them from going mouldy. The Besleys would have been well aware of the necessity to preserve ropes and sails as they were themselves ship owners.

The late Mr. John Besley was the last commercial fisherman at Watchet. He is well remembered for his skill as an accurate forecaster of the weather and his reluctance to let slip any of his vast knowledge of fishing which were after all the trade secrets of generations. But on rare occasions he would relent. The writer occasionally accompanied Mr. Besley to his stake nets on the foreshore at low water, and remembers on one occasion commenting on the large number of small dog whelks which live in abundance among the large pebbles and regretted the fact that they were not of the larger edible species :

"Large whelks can be caught and I will show you how" said John.

Taking a dog fish (he first killed it by striking its head on the wooden

122

John Besley the last of Watchet's commercial fishermen.

(By courtesy Mrs. M. Putt)

stake) from his nets he then carried it towards the sea and on the edge of the tide, placed it under a large flat stone. He explained that the height of the tides would now be reducing and therefore the stone would be under water and inaccessible for about 10 days, by which time the dog fish would be a little riper and irresistable to whelks. Sure enough in about 10 days time, again the dog fish was uncovered and about 20 large whelks could be picked up within a ten foot radius of the 'bait' which was certainly riper! Dog fish must be used for bait said John as most other fish having a soft skin would quickly disintegrate and not remain in place for the long period between each Spring Tide. The writer is not particularly fond of whelks therefore this John Besley secret for catching them is passed on with compliments to any reader who may like to try his luck.

Fred Besley, another member of the family, was an expert at catching prawns. With his six foot wide shovel shaped net he worked the seaweed covered ridges near the low water mark. Fred always went prawning after dark in order not to divulge to others the secret ridges and gullies where he knew the prawns were thickest.

123

Prior to the 1920's most of the fish caught at Watchet was taken to a little building in Mill Lane which was known as the fish house. Here it was sorted and filleted and despatched to various retail outlets. The fishhouse after 1930 was in use for a number of years as a fish and chip shop. It is now used as a store and forms part of the residence of the writer.

Another family much involved in the local fishing industry were the Strongs who like the Besleys lived in Anchor Street and marketed most of the locally caught fish. They kept a supply of dried salt cod known as torag and large bowls of Swansea cockles.

Large quantities of shrimps were also caught and sold locally and even limpets were collected from the rocky foreshore and hawked around the town by two ladies, (Lena Gunny and Dina Webber.)

The smell of limpets cooking in bacon fat with parsley and bread-crumbs was a familiar one in Watchet until the 1930's. These two ladies also collected and sold laver, an edible type of seaweed. The writer however does not consider that either cooked laver known as laverbread or fried limpets are a gastronomic delight.

Probably unique to Watchet and the West Somerset coast was the practice of fishing or hunting for conger eels with the aid of dogs, known as 'Glatting'. The extremely high rise and fall of Spring Tides in the Bristol Channel (said to be the second highest in the world) uncovers a vast amount of foreshore at the time of low water. This reveals rocky ledges of blue lias limestone often covered with seaweed. Many of the overhanging ledges provide crevices and deep holes often situated in a shallow pond and here at times conger eels lie hidden from view quietly waiting for the tide to come in again. Fishermen with long sticks would prod under the ledges and into the holes, also under large flat stone slabs. A prodded conger would rush out of the hole at great speed and would then be clobbered with a hook-shaped iron bar known as a Glathook. Well trained dogs would be used to smell out and mark where a conger was lying thus saving much time in unproductive prodding. Yelping dogs tackling a snapping threshing conger was a regular sport fifty years ago but is now a rare occurrence. Some conger fishermen would raise and wedge up large stone slabs leaving just sufficient room underneath to provide a comfortable new abode for a conger. These man-made conger lairs were referred to as Hovers.

Two of the most popular places for conger hunting with dogs were, and indeed still are accessible only on the highest of spring tides.

One is at *Black Rock* off St. Audries. The other, a similar ridge of rocks, is situated towards Blue Anchor and known as *The Tarr.*

Many parts of the foreshore have names not recorded on charts or maps. For instance, the North Easterly part of the *Fishing Ground* off the harbour was always known as *Skobart* and the more Westerly part *Pennymah.* Like many field names on shore their origin is obscure.

124

Mr Sidney (Dumper) Eveleigh with his prawning net

Some Fishy Stories
from the West Somerset Free Press

June 15, 1861

On June 5th William Besley fisherman of Watchet about 1½ miles out at sea, hooked a large underground shark. He got the shark into his boat and having a small axe used it to despatch the shark which was six ft four inches long. On opening it 23 young sharks from 10 to 12 inches long were found in the body, all alive.

Two days later Mr. Besley caught a male shark, not quite as large. In the course of a few more days the brothers Besley caught seven or eight more sharks measuring from six to seven feet in length.

Nov. 16, 1867

There were big catches of sprats at Watchet, much larger than for some years past. A large quantity was sent to Bristol by rail, nearly a ton to Wellington and over three tons to Taunton in addition to those sold in the neighbourhood.

1886

The Besley brothers caught a monster skate or ray which weighed over two hundredweight and was seven and a half feet from nose to end of tail.

1888

The Besley brothers caught the largest conger eel ever caught at Watchet which weighed over 99 pounds. They were disappointed that it failed to turn the scale at 100 pounds. Honest men — they did not pretend that it did. A fish dealer gave them half a sovereign for the conger and it was put in a huge hamper and consigned to Taunton where a firm of fishmongers put it on show.

The Lifeboat

A 33 ft rowing and sailing self-righting lifeboat named *Joseph Somes* was first stationed at Watchet in 1875. She was succeeded by several other similar boats until the station closed in 1944. Although by no means a busy station the crew always responded immediately to any call, and the boat was at all times kept ready in immaculate order. Low water launching was very difficult necessitating the use of at least eight horses to drag the boat on its heavy carriage through the muddy harbour and then over a very rough and exposed foreshore. Such a launch was recorded in April 1878 when a fearful North Easterly gale was raging in the Channel. A Gloucester trow the *Rose* was seen

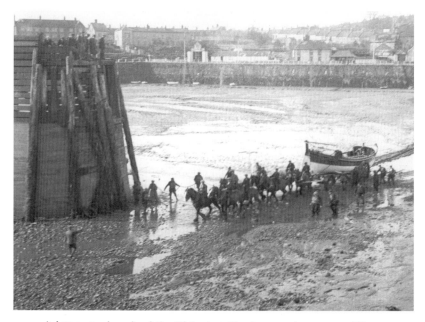

A low water launch of the lifeboat at Watchet was always very difficult and required the use of eight horses to drag it through the muddy harbour. The Lifeboat House with open doors can be seen on the Esplanade.

(By courtesy P. Norton)

to be dragging her anchor about two miles off Watchet and drifting ashore. A man was seen on board and orders were given to launch the lifeboat. Capt. Henry Press undertook to act as coxswain, the appointed coxswain being a much older man and unwell.

It was low tide and the lifeboat with a crew of fourteen had to be pulled through the harbour, then over the rocks and out to the fishing ground, where she was duly launched. Eight horses had been required for this arduous job. Unfortunately the *Rose* drifted onto the rocky shore to the Westward of Warren Limekilns before she could be reached. The lifeboat crew saw the crew of the *Rose* rescued by the coastguards from the shore.

While the lifeboat was lying-to off Blue Anchor waiting for water to return to the harbour, another vessel, the sloop *Olive Branch* of Cardiff was seen to be in difficulties, and was also drifting in shore and showing signals of distress. So the lifeboat beat up to windward and with masterly handling under Captain Press, the crew brought her alongside the sloop, and succeeded in taking off the captain and crew of two. Soon afterwards the vessel dragged her anchors and also went into the rocky shore, quite close to the wreck of the *Rose*.

Watchet's lifeboatmen displayed resourcefulness and great courage in a rescue of two Minehead fishermen in November, 1899.

During darkness, their herring fishing boat – the *Rosalie* – had been driven up Channel by a strong westerly gale and had anchored just to the westward of Watchet Harbour.

It was a bitterly cold night and terrific waves were threatening to swamp their boat. One of the crew of two, due to the intense cold and long exposure was almost helpless. It was impossible, therefore, for the boat to enter harbour without assistance. Despite the noise of the waves and the wind, the men's cries for help were eventually heard ashore.

The lifeboat – *W.H.G. Kingston* – was launched with some difficulty for at the time there was very little depth of water in the harbour, and consequently the boat had to be manhandled through the mud.

When outside the harbour, the heavy lifeboat proved unable to stem the tide. Row as hard as they might the crew could not make headway against the immensely strong flood tide and gale-force head wind.

The lifeboat was gradually forced up channel and away from the boat in distress.

The lifeboat's reserve crew, watching on the west breakwater were greatly concerned as it became obvious the lifeboat was unable to reach the fishing boat in distress. This boat could not be seen, but cries for help were still being faintly heard.

Willie Lee, a reporter for the West Somerset Free Press, and for many years the Hon. Secretary of the Lifeboat was among the watchers on the west breakwater.

127

In a supplement to his paper, he gives his own vivid impressions of the tense atmosphere and the events which followed:

An hour passes with no sign of the lifeboat. Meanwhile the despairing cries of the men in jeopardy continue.

The crowd become additionally anxious, fearing that some disaster has overtaken the lifeboat.

A suggestion is made that a smaller and lighter boat might be able to reach the fishing boat whereas the heavy lifeboat has failed.

Captain's Escott, Wedlake, Davis and A. & S. Nicholas are in consultation.

The sea has moderated slightly and it is thought that if action is to be taken it must be now or never.

Captain Davis gets his small boat with a staff of oars etc., and is immediately joined by the other four Master Mariners.

Captain Escott takes charge and amid tumultuous cheering the brave fellows are off.

For a moment the elements seem determined to check them — an enormous wave striking the piles as the boat's nose comes out into the harbour mouth but they safely emerge through the broken water and pull away.

Being low in the water the wind has not got much of a hold on the boat and she goes through the water at a rate which gladdens the heart of the spectators.

In a minute or two she is lost to sight — a second or so later she re-appears, a black object under the light of the moon's rays, and then disappears.

It seems but a minute or two when she is seen returning, and disappointment is writ large as it is generally conjectured that she has failed in her object.

'She's got 'em' shouts a stentorian voice on the rail of the breakwater, and amid a torrent of cheering from hundreds of throats, the boat returns to the harbour with the two fishermen — John Bryant and George Wills.

They are landed at the breakwater amid a scene of tremendous enthusiasm and are quickly borne off to Mrs Lee's Refreshment Rooms where restoratives and everything necessary are found for the men.

Bryant quickly recovers, but Wills is not so fortunate and it takes a good deal of work on the part of several willing helpers to restore animation to his body and limbs which are almost ice-cold.

Meanwhile the coxswain of the lifeboat (W. Guppy) realising that his lifeboat could not reach the fishing boat, decided to anchor and wait until the tide had slackened.

He and his crew were naturally disappointed when they eventually got to the barely floating fishing boat to find it empty, but on returning to harbour they were relieved to learn the men had been saved.

Laying greased skids on the slipway for return of the lifeboat which is about to be hauled ashore with block and tackle.

No blame, however, could be attached to anyone; coxswain, crew and the Hon. Treasurer who was also in the boat, all did their best, but it was beyond human power to make headway against the frightful sea they encountered.

On rare occasions a particular type of lifeboat supplied to a station would prove to be unsuitable for the conditions in that locality. This would appear to have been the case with the boat at Watchet when as described, it was found to be unsuitable and incapable of reaching the fishing boat in trouble only a short distance from the harbour. The courage, bravery and ability of the men was never in doubt and an award of a pair of binoculars to W. Escott and an aneroid each to A. & S. Nicholas, A. Wedlake and J. Davis the crew who manned the small boat was made by the Institution.

Shortly after this brave rescue by Watchet lifeboatmen albeit in a shore boat, the whole town was outraged when informed by the Lifeboat Authorities that the Watchet station would be closed and a new one would be opened at Minehead. Watchet's pride was wounded and around the harbour unkind and probably untrue words were uttered about Minehead sailors. Meetings were called and brains were racked to produce five Good Reasons why the lifeboat should be retained at Watchet.

So successful was the racking that five extra reasons were produced and

129

these put into print, and sent post-haste to lifeboat H.Q. with a heartfelt appeal for the station to be retained at Watchet *(see page opposite)*.

The Appeal was successful and what was more, Watchet was promised a brand new and improved lifeboat. In 1903 the new lifeboat was ready at a shipyard in London. A Watchet crew sailed her around the coast, a 600 mile journey. She was named the *John Linguard Ross* and was ceremoniously launched at Watchet on Aug 3rd 1903 by Lady Acland Hood. In 1904 she saved the ketch *Annie Christian* and her crew of four.

Although Watchet's boat was not often called for duty, there was a great deal of love and affection for the lifeboat. She was looked on as a safeguard by men who knew the hazards of the sea, and the little community which had lost so many of its sons by shipwreck, felt justified in its fight for its own lifeboat.

A lurking fear that the lifeboat might still be taken away for economic reasons, prompted local folk into organising all sorts of funds raising activities to ensure that the boat was financially self-supporting.

Every year the boat on its carriage would be hauled by horses around the nearby villages and collections made by the sailors.

Occasionally a Regatta would be organised and competing craft included Bristol Channel Pilot Cutters mainly from the Welsh Ports. The last lines of a bit of barely remembered doggerel relating to pilot boats racing at Watchet has been handed down, it runs:

> "As she rounded the mark buoy
> They fired off the gun
> And everyone was happy
> For the little 'Polly' won."

Other harbour sports were an annual event and were often most amusing, usually starting with mud sports such as races, tug of war, and football all played in the mud on the bed of the harbour. When the tide came in very keen rowing and sculling races would take place with the vessels' boats. These would compete with the local coastguards. Wagers were often laid as to who had the fastest boat and some ship's crews would spend hours smoothing down the bottoms of their boats and even polishing them with black lead to make them go faster. Other amusing capers included walking the greasy pole and what was always referred to as a pillow fight consisted of two competitors sitting on the greasy pole and viciously swiping each other not with a pillow but with pig's bladders until one was toppled into the water.

A duck hunt was always in the programme and activities usually ended with a grand battle. Two boats' crews each armed with paper bags of soot or flour would do battle with each other and anyone else who got in the way. All vessels in port dressed ship (hoisted bunting) for the occasion and on shore the town band would help to liven proceedings for 'Lifeboat Day'.

REASONS WHY THE LIFEBOAT SHOULD BE RETAINED AT WATCHET.

1. The Boat was first offered to Minehead and they would have nothing to do with her.

2. The shipping industry is much larger at Watchet :
   14 vessels registered belonging to Minehead.
   38   do.   do.   Watchet.
         gross tonnage   ...   ...   Minehead.
            do.   ...   ...   Watchet.
   43 seamen (manning above) ...   Minehead.
   141   do.   do.   ...   Watchet.

   For the year 1897, the Board of Trade returns for Watchet, " Inward " and " Outward," 845 vessels with 39,007 tonnage.

3. At all times, if necessary, two or three crews could be obtained at Watchet : it is doubtful if one could be obtained at Minehead, for the following reasons : --

   (A) Many of the seamen at Minehead (competent to man the lifeboat) are fishermen, consequently when the fishing boats are at sea, the lifeboat could not be launched if these boats were in distress. In the fishing season the crews leave their vessels to assist at fishing.

   (B) There are not enough seamen at Minehead to man their own vessels. (This is not the case at Watchet.)

   (C) The shipping industry is likely to decrease at Minehead, but at Watchet to be maintained. (The Board of Trade returns show more capital invested in trade, in Watchet, than any other town of its size in Great Britain.)

4. The interest of the seamen of Watchet in the lifeboat and its work is very keen. Three crews were voluntarily raised on the 10th Nov. last : — 1st, for the lifeboat ; 2nd, a crew for the boat which effected the rescue ; 3rd, another crew for the boat which salved the fishing boat in distress.

5. Reports of the District Inspector :—

  9th Dec., 1899—"The boat and house are in remarkably good condition, clean and well kept."

  23rd and 24th April, 1900—"All in splendid order."

The Lifeboat could have done more service in the past if there had been placed here—

  (A) A suitable boat with drop keel.

  (B) Telegraphic communication with other places (this latter has now been done).
    Instances can be given.

The Lifeboat, when summoned, has always been successfully and smartly launched at Watchet. There are places West and East where this could be done (with no outlay) besides being launched *at* Watchet, if need be (no such instance has yet occurred).

The boat is at present placed in the most dangerous part of the coast for vessels :—

  Abreast of Watchet is the Culver Sands, on which several wrecks are recorded.

  To the Eastward are the Gore Sands, where shipping disasters are an annual occurrence.

  Instances—The "Hereford," &c.

The Burnham Boat cannot always get to sea.

The Lifeboat has never been summoned by Minehead during her existence here.

LAUNCHING—The difficulties, at times, at Minehead would be great.

During the 2nd World War, a new motor lifeboat having been stationed at Minehead, orders were received to close both Watchet and Lynmouth lifeboat stations. Their old rowing and sailing lifeboats named *Sarah Pilkington* and *Prichard Frederick Gainer* respectively, were obsolete and the last of their type in the country. Regret and a sense of loss was felt by many when both boats were sent away by rail. Watchet's lifeboat house was later converted into a Public Library by the generosity of Mr. Leonard Stoate.

Although a lifeboat station may be closed the tradition of saving life never dies in a seafaring community, and at Watchet several courageous rescues have since taken place with the use of shore boats. One of these was carried out single-handed by the writers' youngest son Daniel at the age of fourteen. In recognition of this he was awarded an inscribed watch and a Certificate of Thanks by the R.N.L.I.

Watchet Lifeboat en route by road to Blue Anchor (approx. 2 miles) for a practice launch. 1920's.

CHAPTER 10

SAILORS, SHIPWRIGHTS AND HARBOURSIDE CHARACTERS

Watchet's Marine Artist

Thomas Chidgey was born at Watchet in 1855, one of a family long established in the coasting trade and as was usual at that time, he went to sea at an early age in the little smacks and ketches that traded from the harbour. Thomas was gifted at drawing and sketching and from his boyhood he recorded with a pencil or crayon the various ships that entered the port. He also tried painting the various developments of the newly enlarged harbour which he saw at first hand, but his greatest joy was to paint a portrait of a ship at sea in full sail. He excelled at this and must have painted hundreds during his

Thomas Chidgey — Watchet's Marine Artist — a self portrait.
(By courtesy Mr. Adrian Chidgey)

The smack "Thomasine and Mary" later converted to ketch rig. Painting by Thomas Chidgey. *(By courtesy Mrs. N. Gilks)*

lifetime. It is interesting to note on many of Chidgey's paintings that quite large schooners and ketches were steered not with a steering wheel but with a tiller on the open deck. The helmsman was therefore completely exposed in all weather. In fact very few schooners or ketches were fitted with a steering wheel until the early 1900's.

Practically all the ships belonging to Watchet were portrayed on canvas by Thomas and the more he painted the better the result; his ability to illustrate all the intricate and delicate rigging and the sail structure of the various different craft was admitted by critical sea captains. They all, as well as many members of the ships' crew, greatly admired his work and endeavoured to get a painting of their own particular ship to display above the fireplace at home. Visiting sea captains also hearing of his skill would commission a painting of their vessels so that Chidgey's paintings would be taken all around the coasts of the British Isles. Thomas Chidgey probably never got paid very big commissions for his paintings. He painted so many because he enjoyed it, and took great pride in his skill.

He died in 1926 and left behind a rich heritage in the form of a colourful record of the coasting schooners, ketches, brigs and smacks in the last days of sail. Inevitably many of his paintings have been purchased by dealers, but some still remain in the town *(see example on the front cover)*. Several have been presented by the Chidgey family to the Watchet Museum.

Yankee Jack

Watchet's best known and most famous sailor was John Short. Born in 1839 he spent his early days in the local coasting trade, but before he was twenty years of age he, with two other local lads, joined the brig *Promise* which sailed for Cadiz and then on to Quebec. From that time on he was a deep water sailor and voyaged all over the world on a variety of ships. In the 1860's he served on American ships which were engaged in running the blockade of the American Civil War. In 1864 one of these ships the *Levant* transferred to British Registry to escape the attentions of Captain Semmes, the master of the Confederate cruiser Alabama. Because of his service in these ships he was given the nickname of "Yankee Jack" by Watchet sailors.

He sailed over every ocean as an able seaman but his ability and love of singing earned him the role of Solo Chanteyman and in this field he was probably unequalled. He had a very strong but tuneful voice and he added more and more songs learned from various sailors to his repertoire as he sailed on each new ship.

In the late 1800's John Short returned to Watchet to look after his ailing wife and in 1914 he was 'discovered' by Cecil Sharp the famous collector of English Folk Songs & Chanties, to whom he contributed a very varied and valuable selection of authentic songs of the seamen. Later he was visited by another well-known collector of folk songs, Sir Richard Terry, who also recorded the music and words willingly sung again and again by John Short.

He became a hobbler and occasionally sailed again as mate in the local coasting vessels. Because of his powerful voice he was appointed Town Crier by the local Court Leet. It was said that on a quiet day his voice could be heard at Doniford nearly two miles away.

He was also appointed Captain of the local fire brigade by the newly formed Urban Council. There was no fire engine as such only a hand cart to carry the hydrant stand pipe and a few rolls of hose pipe and this simple fire fighting equipment was at first kept in the old lock-up jail, formerly used for drunken sailors, situated under the stone steps of the Market House.

Most deep-water sailors and many of those in the coasting trade were quite skilled at sennett and decorative ropework, and would take great pride in making intricate handles or beckets for their sea chests. One of the beckets from John Short's sea chest is owned by the writer and is a beautiful example of its type. After he came ashore John still kept his hand in and spent many hours with Capt. John Binding making decorative sennett door mats from old rope.

Some of the chanties collected by Sharpe and Terry are well-known today and are often sung in schools and by folk groups. They include such old favourites as A. Rovin', Rio Grande, and Shenondoa.

As a small boy the writer attended a concert held at the local Baptist Church Schoolroom and remembers John Short walking up to the stage to entertain his friends and neighbours. John was then over ninety years of age, white haired and frail, but upright and proud. He disdainfully brushed aside some well meaning ladies who attempted to arm him up the steps to the stage. Here he really burst forth with a surprisingly powerful rendering of a sea chanty and also a lovely old song called The Sweet Nightingale. This song, although not a sea chanty, would appear to have been a favourite of his for it is on record that he once sang it at a meeting of the Watchet Court Leet held at its traditional meeting place, the Bell Inn.

Cecil Sharpe was very appreciative and grateful for John Short's help and his contributions to his collection of Sea Chanties for he wrote of him as follows:

"Although seventy six years of age, he is apparently so far as physical activity and mental alertness go, still in the prime of life. He has too the folk singer's tenacious memory and although I am sure he does not know it, a very great musical ability of the uncultivated unconscious order. He now holds the office of Town Crier in his native town, presumably on account of his voice which is rich, resonant and powerful, and yet so flexible that he can execute trills, turns and graces with a delicacy and finish that would excite the envy of many a professional vocalist.

Mr. Short has spent more than fifty years in sailing ships and throughout the greater part of his career, was a recognised chantyman, i.e. solo singer who led the chanty's. It would be difficult, I imagine, to find a more experienced exponent of the art of chanty singing and I account myself particularly fortunate in having made his acquaintance in the course of my investigations and won his generous assistance.

Some of the chanties sung by John Short at Watchet.

Leave her Johnny, leave her.	Bully in the alley.
The hog eyed man.	Liza Lee.
Do let me go gels.	Haul on the bowline.
Whip Jamboree.	Paddy Doyle.
Roll and Go.	Knock a man down.
Roller Boller.	Round the corner Sally.
Huckleberry Hunting.	So handy.
O Johnny come to Hilo.	Cheerly man.
Good morning ladies all.	The sailor likes his bottle o.
The bully boat is coming.	The dead horse.
Stormalong John.	Bonny was a warrior.
Lucy Long.	Blow boys come blow together.
The Black Ball line.	A hundred years on the Eastern shore.
Fire Fire.	Won't you go my way.
Heave away my Johnny.	O Billy Riley.
Haul away Joe.	Tom is gone to Hilo.

137

John Short, Watchet's most famous sailor.　　*(By courtesy Mr. G. Attiwell)*

Poor old Reuben Ranzo.	Tommy's gone away.
General Taylor.	Sing fare you well.
Paddy works on the railway.	Walk him along Johnny.
Blow ye winds of morning.	One more day.
Rio Grand.	Shallow brown.
Let the bullgine run.	Hanging Johnny.
Old Stormy.	

John Short lived until he was 94 and was active and singing until just a few weeks before his death in 1933.

An Obituary notice in *The Times* so rightly said of Watchet's old sailor who had contributed such a wealth of music and song for posterity:

"He thought little of his reputation as a singer but much more of homely things."

The following verses were written by the late Alfred John Short of Watchet and recited by him soon after John Short's death at an annual meeting of Watchet's Court Leet held at the Bell Inn.

JOHN SHORT — 1839-1933

There were many fine men born in this Town,
Who brought it much credit and renown,
Among the young sailors who left this small Port,
Was a notable figure, his name was John Short.

His home was a cottage, close to the quay,
And there he developed his love of the sea.
With two boyhood friends named "Chidgey & Smith"
In a barque called "The Promise" he sailed for Cadiz.

Then across the Atlantic to far off Quebec
With his lust for adventure by danger unchecked,
The sea was his life, his life was the sea
And a confident faith in his own destiny.

To Valparaiso in a barque "The Hugh Block"
In rounding the "Horn" John got a great shock
Tempestuous seas, with winds of gale force
Made the vessel unmanageable, miles off course.

After six weeks of horror they limped into port
And John had adventures of a far different sort.
In the great "Civil War" he supported each cause,
Evading their rigorous Maritime laws.

139

A lover of "shanties" with a deep sonorous voice,
He oft led the seamen in songs of their choice.
As they hauled on the Capstan they lustily sang
And over the waves the harmony rang.

But the call of the homeland, and his sick ailing wife,
Brought him back to her bedside where she fought for her life.
He lived out his days in his little home port
And was made "Bellman Crier" by this ancient Court.

A mutual friendship with the late Cecil Sharpe
Who was thrilled with the voice of this "Nautical Bard"
As John sang his shanties with vocal dexterity
Sharpe recorded the lyrics, in trust for Posterity.

The Baptist Church he always attended
Each Sabbath Day, his way he wended,
Whatever the weather, in sunshine or rain
John's voice would be heard in each joyous refrain.

When he reached the age of ninety-four
We knew we'd hear his voice no more.
The sad news spread, both near and far,
John Short, at last, had "Crossed the Bar"

A.J.S.

It is gratifying to know that John Short's little cottage near the harbour is in a Conservation Area and has recently been renovated by its owner who appreciates local maritime history. The name-plate "Yankee Jack's Cottage" will help to keep alive the story of Watchet's famous old sailor.

It would be impossible to mention all Watchet Sailors in this book. Quite a number went "DEEP WATER" in ocean going ships which traded from large ports. At Watchet museum is a most interesting print of the Clipper Ship *Lady Melville,* 1,100 tons of London, which is depicted passing through icebergs on her homeward voyage from Melbourne on May 21st 1863. This ship was commanded by Capt. H. Gimblett of Watchet. Also serving aboard the *Lady Melville* was a young midshipman from Minehead. His name was John Kent Ridler who later in his career was to take command of the *Orient,* one of the first liners of the famous *Orient Line.* Another painting of the large four-masted barque *Arrocan* of Liverpool is also on view; she also traded to the Far East under the command of Capt. Turner, a Watchet man. Capt. Henry Press who was born in 1844 had close family ties with Watchet. He was a first class Bristol Channel pilot who mainly tended the larger ships bound for the Bridgwater river. He boarded them from his little sailing cutter which he sometimes based at Watchet.

In 1879 he emigrated to Auckland, New Zealand and from there he sailed to Melbourne, Australia in his cutterlike yacht the *Taniwha* to take part in a Regatta. He decided to settle at Williamstown, near Melbourne and entered the Victorian Pilotage Service in which he remained for 26 years. Capt. Press was also a successful artist and produced many fine sea-scapes. A large painting of his, depicting a Watchet lifeboat rescue, can be seen at Watchet Council Office, unfortunately it is too large to be hung in the Museum. Capt. Press was joined in Australia by Capt. Alfred Nicholas of Watchet and his son Harold. The latter was later to become harbourmaster of Freemantle.

Another ship's master of interest was Capt. Wake who spent most of his life in steam ships in the China seas. He returned to Watchet, his home town, on his retirement, c. 1920.

On his living-room wall he displayed his sword which he had used on more than one occasion to prevent his ship being taken over by Chinese pirates.

Even today Watchet men can still be found in command of large ocean-going ships.

Ben Williams (shipwright)

Michael Bouquet, the authoritive West Country marine historian and author, has included much of the story of this Watchet shipwright in his book "No Gallant Ship".

Born at Watchet in 1838 Ben served his apprenticeship under George Escott Geen and later worked at one of the Bridgwater shipyards. Almost certainly he was in Watchet helping to build *The Star of the West* in 1859. This was the last ship to be built at Watchet.

As previously explained, the shipbuilding site was destroyed by the new harbour development and prospects for a young and ambitious shipwright who wished to marry, were not very promising. In 1861 therefore Ben left the country in the full rigged ship *Queen of England.* He was engaged as ship's carpenter and voyaged to China and then on to Australia, where he left the ship with his tools, his clothes and half-a-guinea in his pocket. He worked for a shipbuilder in Sydney for some time, then sailed to Portland, Oregan, U.S.A. While there, he built some of the first craft to ascend the Columbia River. He became foreman shipwright for a firm trading on the river and earned a very good salary.

In 1867 he returned to Watchet to marry, his capital of 10/6d by now increased to £900, a small fortune in those days, he decided to set up in business on his own. In 1868 he took on the completion of the ketch *Argo* which was under construction at Swansea for John Ridler and Capt. Pulsford of Minehead. Robert Vanstone who had started building the vessel had gone bankrupt.

In 1869 he submitted plans and applied to the Watchet Harbour Commissioners to build a graving dock in the corner of the harbour near the

Ben Williams, Watchet Shipwright. *(Courtesy of Michael Bouquet)*

London Inn at his own expense. He was authorised to build the dock at a yearly ground rental of £6 but it was stipulated that he should agree to the dock being open to all other shipbuilders according to their stem (turn) at a charge not exceeding 5/- for 24 hours including the use by such other ship-builders of the said Benjamin Williams, capstan, and other fixed machinery (if any).

The writer has been handed the original plan of the proposed graving dock which was signed and submitted by Ben Williams to the Harbour Commissioners in Dec. 1869. It was to be 100 ft long by 47 ft at its widest point which would be about right for the size of ships using Watchet at that time.

There is no evidence that this graving dock was ever built. Possibly because of the conditions that applied, Watchet's small ship-building industry was therefore doomed.

Ben invested some of his capital in a schooner called the *Princess* which had been built at Prince Edward Island in 1863. He also constructed a small steam yacht in 1878 called the *Florence* and possibly may have been the builder of the small trawler for the Besley family which was called the *Lily Green.*

In 1881 Ben had completed the building of a beautiful schooner at Mine-

142

head; she was called the *Perriton* and was owned by Thomas Kent Ridler of Minehead. This fine ship was eventually sunk by gunfire from a German submarine in 1918.

After completion of the *Perriton*, Ben left Watchet and took employment with the Orient Line at the Royal Albert Dock, London and then at Tilbury for the same company where he was made foreman shipwright.

In 1906 he retired and lived at Barry which is opposite Watchet on the Welsh side of the Bristol Channel. On occasions he sailed across to his home town in a sailing boat built by himself and believed to be called *Tipperary*. He died in 1931.

Another little sailing boat built by him entirely of oak, and named *Phyllis* after his grand-daughter, eventually came into the hands of the writer at Watchet. It was much admired by many, for its good appearance and the obvious skilled workmanship of its builder.

A beautifully made half model of a boat made by Ben Williams, and believed to be of either the aforementioned *Tipperary* or the *Phyllis*, is on display in Watchet's museum.

Three other shipwrights known of by the writer were George Passmore, who was owner of the ill-fated brig *Princess Royal*, Neil Besley whose *Adze* is also in the museum, and William Jones whose workshop and yard were situated in Esplanade Lane until the 1930's.

The schooner on the right, in Minehead Harbour, is the "Perriton", built at Minehead in 1881 by Ben Williams, a Watchet shipwright. The ketch "Argo" on the left was also built by him at Swansea, for the Riddler family of Minehead. The whitewashed building is the old Customs house.
(By courtesy Michael Bouquet)

143

Bob Williams

Said to be a relative of Ben Williams was one Bob Williams. Not such a notable man as Ben, but nevertheless an interesting and amusing little story has been handed down by those interested in harbour lore.

It seems that Bob kept a small holding but also helped in the loading and unloading of ships. Some of the ships brought wheat from overseas for use in Stoate's Flour Mills; much of it came from France. On one occasion a cargo of sacks of Russian wheat was brought in from Danzig. It was the custom that dockers would sweep up any loose and dirty wheat which might otherwise be left in the hold of the ship and this they usually took home to feed their chickens. Bob however decided to sow his dirty Danzig wheat in his small holding. In due course the Russian wheat broke through the ground but it was accompanied by hundreds of pretty little weeds which had never been seen at Watchet before. Many people gathered around to see the pretty weeds and laughingly gave them the name of Bob Williams Weeds.

By the next year however they had stopped laughing for the weeds had spread into all the adjoining fields and gardens. The name of the weed was rapidly altered to "That Bloody Bob Williams Weed". Some years later apparently it had spread over the hill to the little town of Williton but was known by the gardeners there as "That Bloody Watchet Weed". It still flourishes at Watchet and is probably still spreading all over the country under various names.

Subsequent enquiries to the Somerset College of Agriculture & Horticulture have ascertained that the correct name for the weed is Annual Mercury (a relative of Dog's Mercury). Miss Caroline Giddens, an authority on local wild plants and flowers, confirms that Annual Mercury was not known in West Somerset until the 1880's.

That "Bloody Bob Williams" Weed

144

Ships leaving harbour would of necessity have to take aboard food stuffs that would keep for some time. In particular bread could be used for only a limited time before it would go stale and mouldy. Hard biscuits were therefore carried and used when the bread was uneatable. These biscuits known as sea biscuits or hard tack could be obtained at any of the big ports around the coast but Watchet had its own brand of biscuits which were claimed to be much superior to those sold elsewhere. Visiting as well as local ships would always stock up with Celebrated Watchet Biscuits and indeed they became quite famous.

Basking in this fame were the two rival confectioners, Louie Hole of Market Street and William Besley of Mill Street and of course Messrs. Stoate who milled and supplied the local flour.

There were other bakers confections which were produced almost exclusively in the towns of Watchet, and Bridgwater. They were known as Manchips; oval-shaped and of Croissant-like texture, when split down the middle, buttered and served hot, they were delicious. Watchet's Manchips were produced by the long established bakery in Mill Street owned by the Besley family. Thus once again we find a curious link between Bridgwater and Watchet, again involving the Besley family of Huguenot descent. Could it be that the Besley family brought the recipe for the mouth-watering Manchips from the Continent to Somerset? Sad to relate "Manchips" and also "Fatcakes" (another local confection) seem to have lost favour in recent years and can no longer be found in Watchet shops. Both confections were certainly available in the 1940's and 50's. Long before that they were often consumed in large quantities at Watchet celebrations of *Caturns Night.*

This quaint old custom from the dim and distant past was generally thought to have been initiated by a Queen Catherine (no one knows which) who, after visiting a local cloth making establishment, boarded ship and sailed from the port.

Before leaving Queen Catherine (or Caturn to Watchet folk) was said to have generously provided a feast for everyone of "Hot cakes and Cider". The treat was so enjoyed that it was decided to make it an annual event. Every year after that, late in November, folk would gather of an evening to partake of a similar feast. While munching their delicious fatcakes and manchips helped down by noggins of Farmhouse Cider (Scrumpy) they would look forward to their next festive occasion at Christmas, and altogether would recite the following jolly little jingle:

> Tis Caturns Night
> We do believe
> And tomorrow month
> Be Christmas Eve.
> Hoo ray — Hoo ray — Hoo ray.

145

As before mentioned, the famous poet Coleridge, was thought to have composed the *Ryme of the Ancient Mariner* after talking to old sailors on the pier at Watchet in 1798.

The poem vividly conveys the superstitious fears of men of the sea at that time. Even until the turn of the last century there were still old sailors at Watchet who watched for bad omens and who had a lurking fear of Witchcraft. Many of them feared a phenomenon known as St. Elmo's Fire, which we know now is caused by certain atmospheric conditions and which would on rare occasions, be seen glowing at a ship's masthead. This was considered an unlucky omen for those on board and foretold death.

It was believed by some sailors that when their ship was becalmed, a breeze of wind could be induced by stabbing a knife into the ships main mast.

Another superstitious custom was to cast some coins overboard and thus buy some wind from "DOWN BELOW".

A run of bad luck on a vessel, was often blamed on either someone aboard who was said to be a Jonah or on someone ashore who had "put the toads" (i.e. cast a spell) on the ship. Around 1890, an old lady who lived with her son Sammy near the harbour, was believed to have certain uncanny powers. Sea Captains were aware of this and as she was a pipe smoker and also enjoyed a tot of brandy, she was usually kept well supplied as an insurance against her reputed ability to cast a spell.

Captain Bray, master of the schooner *Forest Deer,* was one man who regretted not treating her with due respect. His vessel was under repair alongside the West Pier, a new spar had been fitted and the old one was laying on the pier. The Captain intended taking it home for burning. The old lady had other ideas and was soon making off with it. Captain Bray called her a thief, and insisted that she left the spar on the pier, whereupon she warned him of her ability to 'whistle up the wind'. Perhaps the Captain should have heeded her warning but he did not give way. On his very next trip terrible weather was encountered, the new spar was ripped out by the wind and the *Forest Deer* was nearly wrecked. On every subsequent voyage he also encountered gale force winds.

Another ex master mariner who felt uneasy and apprehensive about the reputed powers of the same old lady was her neighbour Captain Chidgey, landlord of the London Inn, for shortly after he had angered her by refusing to serve her a tot of brandy on the slate (i.e. on credit), he discovered his pony had suddenly and mysteriously dropped dead.

Were these strange happenings involving mature sea-faring men just coincidence? Maybe they were, but in Captain Bray's case his nerve cracked and he had to give up his career at sea.

The pony dropped dead

Watchet Nicknames

By the 1930's, the sailing ships having almost disappeared, dozens of sailors would be seen ashore, pacing up and down in Market Street, or standing talking, in little groups either on the Esplanade, or at the entrance to the West Pier known as Quay Court. They are well remembered by the writer. Many of them wore the traditional dark blue Appledore frocks or jerseys and little soft topped peaked caps. Most of them had a great sense of humour, and some excelled at spinning yarns, which at times caused those listening to roll about laughing helplessly.

Many of the sailors and longshoremen of character had been given nicknames by their shipmates and some of these nicknames were even handed down from father to son.

Anyone walking around the harbour at that time would have been sure to hear tales of "Old Bottles", "Teddy Slackass" or "Margerine Jack", the latter an old sea captain was awarded his nickname by his crew who considered him to be rather tight when victualling his ship. "Bob the Devil", "Shackles" and "Bouncy" could often be seen on the pier, and on the Esplanade one might well pass the time of day with "Billy Go Deeper", "Wacka Beans" or even "The King of Lundy." The so-called King was an eccentric gentleman of independent means who had come to reside in the town. In the early 1900's he journeyed to London where he attended at an important property auction, Lundy Island was up for sale. The King outbid everyone else and returned to Watchet, where he promised the freedom of the Island to all Watchet sailors. He also bestowed Knighthoods on a couple of Sea Captains. His friend Henry Davey the local grocer was similarly honoured and bid to "Rise Sir Henry, Knight of Lundy Island". Unfortunately it transpired that the King had insufficient financial backing to complete the purchase and the deal fell through. Later he always carried a walking stick and would lash out viciously at boys who mischievously called after him.

"Fearless Joe" was not a sailor, he was the local barber but was given the nickname by the sailors who were very proud of him. The story goes that a travelling circus came to town in the early 1900's and was situated on the cliff top site above the harbour. As a publicity stunt the local barber was offered £5 if he would shave the lion tamer in the lion's cage which would contain six ferocious lions. £5 was a lot of money in those days and Joseph Colwell the barber, a normally quiet little man surprisingly agreed to take on the job. Great publicity was given and the whole town turned up expecting to see Joe eaten by the lions. This did not happen. Joe was quite calm and shaved the tamer perfectly without batting an eyelid. After the show however, the circus manager could not be found and no £5 was forthcoming and as the circus was starting to pack up, Joe called on the sailors for their support. A large gang made their way to the site and threatened a rough house. Joe was promptly paid his £5 and, hero that he was, paid for drinks all round for the sailors.

"Fearless Joe" also occasionally took part with others in a traditional and quaint old Watchet custom known as

PUTTING UP THE BROOM

whenever it became known to pranksters such as Joe that a man's wife was away from home, the mischievous prank of "Putting up the broom" was liable to take place. During darkness while the lonely husband slept, a sweeping brush or broom was likely to be tied to the chimneypot or high on the eaves of his house, a conspicuous notice would be displayed reading "Housekeeper wanted" or "Half a bed to let". Sometimes, probably at the instigation of womenfolk, a broom and notice would appear on houses of eligible bachelors.

Old Bottles was a hobbler with a doubtful claim to fame, and perhaps infamous would better describe some of his alleged deeds. According to Bert Bale, a member of the lifeboat crew, and a notorious story-teller, Old Bottles would persist in eating fried limpets which were liable at times to cause him uncontrollable flatulence. Bert declared that whenever Old Bottles broke wind at his cottage in West Street the reports could be heard at the lifeboat house over 400 yards away. Bert's stories however were known at times to be exaggerated, and he was not entirely believed when he further declared,